Sleeping Beauty and Other
Prose Fancies

SLEEPING BEAUTY AND OTHER PROSE FANCIES

BY

RICHARD LE GALLIENNE

JOHN LANE: THE BODLEY HEAD
LONDON AND NEW YORK
1900

COPYRIGHT, 1900
BY JOHN LANE
All rights reserved

UNIVERSITY PRESS · JOHN WILSON
AND SON · CAMBRIDGE, U.S.A.

TO

CLEMENT SHORTER,

WITH ADMIRATION OF A COURAGEOUS CRITICAL
GIFT TOO RARELY EMPLOYED, AND
IN FRIENDSHIP.

CONTENTS

		PAGE
I.	SLEEPING BEAUTY	1
II.	A LITERARY OMNIBUS	11
III.	THE SILVER GIRL	16
IV.	WORDS WRITTEN TO MUSIC	24
V.	AT ELIM ARE TWELVE WELLS	35
VI.	THE BLUE JAR	41
VII.	A DANISH BATHING PLACE	48
VIII.	AN AFFECTIONATE LETTER FROM TABBY	55
IX.	DESIDERIUM	61
X.	THE SECOND COMING OF THE IDEAL	63
XI.	A DESULTORY NOTE ON VALUES	95
XII.	SO THIS IS AMERICA!	103
XIII.	POETRY AND THE JUBILEE	120
XIV.	THE LESSON OF ROMEIKE	131
XV.	CONCERNING A DEFINITION OF POETRY	143

CONTENTS

		PAGE
XVI.	THE DETHRONING OF STEVENSON	151
XVII.	A NEW WOMAN POET	161
XVIII.	MR. STEPHEN PHILLIPS' POETRY	170
XIX.	TRAGEDY AND MR. WILLIAM WATSON	181
XX.	*A Propos* THE BROWNING LOVE-LETTERS	192
XXI.	HUBERT CRACKANTHORPE	200

SLEEPING BEAUTY

"Every woman is a sleeping beauty," I said, sententiously.

"Only some need more waking than others?" replied my cynical friend.

"Yes, some will only awaken at the kiss of great love or great genius, which are not far from the same thing," I replied.

"I see," said the gay editor with whom I was talking.

Our conversation was of certain authors of our acquaintance, and how they managed their inspiration, of what manner were their muses, and what the methods of their stimulus. Some, we had noted, throve on constancy, to others inconstancy was the lawless law of their being; and so accepted had become these indispensable conditions of their literary activity that the wives had long since ceased to be jealous of the other wives. To a household dependent on poetry, constancy in many cases would mean poverty, and certain good literary wives had been known to rate their husbands with a lazy and unproductive faithfulness. The editor sketched a tragic *ménage* known to him, where the husband, a lyric poet of fame, had become so chronically devoted to his despairing wife that destitution stared them in the face. It was in vain that she implored him, with tears in her eyes, to fall in love with some other woman. She, she alone, he said, must be his inspiration; but as the domesticated muse is too often a muse of exquisite silence, too happy to sing its happiness, this lawful passion, which might otherwise have been turned to account, was unproductive too.

"And such a pretty woman," said the editor, sympathetically. Of another happier case of domestic hallucination, he made the remark: "Says he owes it all to his wife! and you never saw such a plain woman in your life."

"How do you know she is plain?" I asked; "may n't it be that the husband's sense of beauty is finer than yours? Do you think all beauty is for all men? or that the beauty all can see is best worth seeing?"

SLEEPING BEAUTY

And then we spoke the words of wisdom and wit which I have written in ebony on the lintel of this little house of words. He who would write to live must talk to write, and I confess that I took up this point with my friend, and continued to stick to it, no doubt to his surprise, because I had at the moment some star-dust on the subject nebulously streaming and circling through my mind, which I was anxious to shape into something of an ordered world. So I talked not to hear myself speak, but to hear myself think, — always, I will anticipate the malicious reader in saying, an operation of my mind of delightful unexpectedness.

"Why! you're actually thinking," chuckles one's brain to itself, "go on. Dance while the music's playing;" and so the tongue goes dancing with pretty partners of words, till suddenly one's brain gives a sigh, the wheels begin to slow down, and music and dancing stop together, till some chance influence, a sound, a face, a flower, how or whence we know not, comes to wind it up again.

The more one ponders the mystery of beauty, the more one realises that the profoundest word in the philosophy of æsthetics is that of the simple-subtle old proverb: Beauty is in the eyes of the beholder. Beauty, in fact, is a collaboration between the beholder and the beheld. It has no abstract existence, and is visible or invisible as one has eyes to see or not to see it, that is, as one is endowed or not endowed with the sense of beauty, an hieratic sense which, strangely enough, is assumed as common to humanity. Particularly is this assumption made in regard to the beauty of women. Every man, however beauty-blind he may really be, considers himself a judge of women — though he might hesitate to call himself a judge of horses. Far indeed from its being true that the sense of beauty is universal, there can be little doubt that the democracy is for the most part beauty-blind, and that while it has a certain indifferent pleasure in the comeliness that comes of health, and the prettiness that goes with ribbons, it dislikes and fears that finer beauty which is seldom comely, never pretty, and always strange.

National galleries of art are nothing against this truth. Once in awhile the nation may rejoice over the purchase of a bad picture it can understand, but for the most part — what to it are all these strange pictures, with their disquieting colours and haunted faces? What recks the nation at large of its Bellinis or its Botticellis? what even of its Titians or its Tintorettos? Was it not the few who bought them, with the money of the many, for the delight of the few?

Well, as no one would dream of art-criticism by *plébiscite*, why should universal conventions of the beauty of women find so large an acceptance merely because they are universal? There are vast multitudes, no doubt, who deem the scented-soap beauties of Bouguereau more beautiful than the strange ladies of Botticelli, and, were you to inquire, you would discover that your housemaid wonders to herself, as she dusts your pictures to the sound of music-hall song, what you can see in the plain lean women of Burne-Jones, or the repulsive ugliness of "The Blessed Damosel." She thanks heaven that she was not born with such a face, as she takes a reassuring glance in the mirror at her own regular prettiness, and more marketable bloom.

For, you see, this beauty is still asleep for her — as but a few years ago it was asleep for all but the artists who first kissed it awake.

All beauty was once asleep like that, even the very beauty your housemaid understands and perhaps exemplifies. It lay asleep awaiting the eye of the beholder, it lay asleep awaiting the kiss of genius; and, just as one day nothing at all seemed beautiful, so some day all things will come to seem so, if the revelation be not already complete.

For indeed much beauty that was asleep fifty years ago has been passionately awakened, and given a sceptre and a kingdom since then: the beauty of lonely neglected faces that no man loved, or loved only by stealth, for fear of the mockery of the blind; the beauty of unconventional contours and unpopular colouring, the beauty of pallor, of the red-haired, and the *fausse maigre*. The fair and the fat are no longer paramount, and the beauty of forty has her day.

Nor have the discoveries of beauty been confined to the faces and forms of women. In Nature too the waste places where no man sketched or golfed have been reclaimed for the kingdom of beauty. The little hills had not really rejoiced us till Wordsworth came, but we had learnt his lesson so well that the beauty of the plain slept for us all the longer, till with Tennyson and Millet it awakened at last, — the beauty of desolate levels, solitary moorlands, and the rich melancholy of the fens.

Wherever we turn our eyes, we find the beauty of character supplanting the beauty of form, or, if not supplanting, asserting its claim to a place beside the haughty sister who would fain keep Cinderella, red-headed and *retroussée*, in the background — yes! and for many even supplanting! It is only when regularity of form and personal idiosyncrasy and intensity of character are united in a face, that the so-called classical beauty is secure of holding its own with those whose fealty most matters — and that union to any triumphant degree is exceedingly rare. Even when that union has come about there are those, in this war of the classicism and romanticism of faces, who would still choose the face dependent on pure effect for its charm; no mask of unchanging beauty, but a beauty whose very life is change, and whose magic, so to say, is a miraculous accident, elusive and unaccountable.

Miraculous and unaccountable! In a sense all beauty is that, but in the case of the regular, so to say, authorized beauty, it seems considerably less so. For in such faces, the old beauty-masters will tell you, the brow is of such a breadth and shape, the nose so long, the mouth shaped in this way, and the eyes set and coloured in that; and thus, of this happy marriage of proportions, beauty has been born. This they will say in spite of the everyday fact of thousands of faces being thus proportioned and coloured without the miracle taking place, ivory lamps in which no light of beauty burns. And it is this fact that proves the truth of the newer beauty we are considering. Form is thus seen to be dependent on expression, though expression, the new beauty-masters would contend, is independent of form. For the new beauty there are no such rules; it is, so to say, a prose beauty, for which there is no formulated prosody, entirely free and individual in its rhythms, and personal in its effects. Sculpture is no longer its chosen voice among the arts, but rather music with its myriad meanings, and its infinitely responsive inflections.

You will hear it said of such beauty — that it is striking, individual, charming, fascinating and so on, but not exactly beautiful. This, if you are an initiate of the new beauty, you will resist, and permit no other description but beauty — the only word which accurately expresses the effect made upon you. That such effect is not produced upon others need not depress you; for similarly you might say of the beauty that others applaud that for you it seems attractive, handsome, pretty, dainty and so on, but not exactly beautiful; or admitting its beauty, that it is but one of many types of beauty, the majority of which are neither straight-lined nor regular.

For when it is said that certain faces are not exactly beautiful, what is meant is that they fail to conform to one or other of the straight-lined types; but by what authority has it been settled once and for all that beauty cannot exist outside the straight line and the chubby curve? It matters not what authority one were to bring, for vision is the only authority in this matter, and the more ancient the authority the less is it final, for it has thus been unable to take account of all the types that have come into existence since its day, types spiritual, intellectual, and artistic, born of the complex experience of the modern world.

And yet it has not been the modern world alone that has awakened that beauty independent of, and perhaps greater than, the beauty of form and colour; rather it may be said to have reawakened it by study of certain subtle old masters of the Renaissance; and the great beauties who have made the tragedies and love-stories of the world, so far as their faces have been preserved to us, were seldom "beautiful," as the populace would understand beauty. For perhaps the highest beauty is visible only to genius, or that great love which, we have said, is a form of genius. It was only, it will be remembered, at the kiss of a prince that Sleeping Beauty might open her wonderful eyes.

A LITERARY OMNIBUS

THERE were ten of us travelling life's journey together from Oxford Circus to the Bank, one to fall away early at Tottenham Court Road, leaving his place unfilled till we steamed into Holborn at Mudie's, where, looking up to make room for a new arrival, I perceived, with an unaccustomed sense of being at home in the world, that no less than four of us were reading. It became immediately evident that in the new arrival our reading party had made an acquisition, for he carried three books in a strap, and to the fourth, a dainty blue cloth volume with rough edges, he presently applied a paper-knife with that eager tenderness which there is no mistaking. The man was no mere lending library reader. He was an aristocrat, a poet among readers, a bookman *pur sang*. We were all more or less of the upper crust ourselves, with the exception of a dry and dingy old gentleman in the remote corner who, so far as I could determine, was deep in a digest of statutes. His interest in the new-comer was merely an automatic raising of the head as the 'bus stopped, and an automatic sinking of it back again as we once more rumbled on. The rest of us, however, were not so poorly satisfied. This fifth reader to our coach had suddenly made us conscious of our freemasonry, and henceforward there was no peace for us till we had, by the politest stratagems of observation, made out the titles of the books from which as from beakers our eyes were silently and strenuously drinking such different thoughts and dreams.

The lady third from the door on the side facing me was reading a book which gave me no little trouble to identify, for she kept it pressed on her lap with tantalising persistence, and the headlines, which I was able to spell out with eyes grown telescopic from curiosity, proved those tiresome headlines which refer to the contents of chapter or page instead of considerately repeating the title of the book. It was not a novel. I could tell that, for there wasn't a scrap of conversation, and it wasn't novelist's type. I watched like a lynx to catch a look at the

A LITERARY OMNIBUS

binding. Suddenly she lifted it up, I cannot help thinking out of sheer kindness, and it proved to be a stately unfamiliar edition of a book I should have known well enough, simply *The French Revolution*. Why will people tease one by reading Carlyle in any other edition but the thin little octavos, with the sticky brown and black bindings of old?

The pretty dark-haired girl next but one on my own side what was she reading? No! ... But, she was, really!

Need I say that my eyes beat a hasty retreat to my little neighbour, the new-comer, who sat facing me next to the door, one of whose books in the strap I had instantly recognised as *Weir of Hermiston*. Of the other two, one was provokingly turned with the edges only showing, and of the edges I couldn't be quite sure, though I was almost certain they belonged to an interesting new volume of poems I knew of. The third had the look of a German dictionary. But, of course, it was the book he was reading that was the chief attraction, and I rather like to think that probably I was the only one of his fellow travellers who succeeded in detecting the honey-pot from which he was delicately feeding. It took me some little time, though the book, with its ribbed blue cover gravely lined with gold and its crisp rose-yellow paper, struck me with instant familiarity. "Preface to Second Edition," deciphered backwards, was all I was able to make out at first, for the paper-knife loitered dreamily among the opening pages, till at last with the turning of a page, the prose suddenly gave place to a page prettily broken up with lines and half-lines of italics, followed by a verse or two — and "Of course," I exclaimed to myself, with a curious involuntary gratitude. "It is Dr. Wharton's *Sappho*."

And so it was. That penny 'bus was thus carelessly carrying along the most priceless of written words. We were journeying in the same conveyance with

"*Like the sweet apple which reddens upon the topmost bough,*
 A-top on the topmost twig — which the pluckers forgot somehow —
Forgot it not, nay, but got it not, for none could get it till now;"

with

"*I loved thee, Atthis, long ago;*"

with

"The moon has set, and the Pleiades; it is midnight, the time is going by, and I sleep alone."

Yes, it was no less a presence than Sappho's that had stepped in amongst us at the corner of New Oxford Street. Visibly it had been a little black-bearded bookman, rather French in appearance, possibly a hard-worked teacher of languages — but actually it had been Sappho. So strange are the contrasts of the modern world, so strange the fate of beautiful words. Two thousand five hundred years! So far away from us was the voice that had suddenly called to us, a lovely apparition of sound, as we trundled dustily from Oxford Circus to the Bank.

"The moon has set, and the Pleiades; it is midnight, the time is going by, and I sleep alone," I murmured, as the conductor dropped me at Chancery Lane.

THE SILVER GIRL

SOMETIMES when I have thought that the Sphinx's mouth is cruel, and could not forget its stern line for all her soft eyes, I have reassured myself with the memory of a day when I saw it so soft and tender with heavenly pity, that I could have gone down on my knees then and there by the side of the luncheon table, where the champagne was already cooling in the ice-pail, and worshipped her — would have done so had I thought such public worship to her taste. It was no tenderness to me, but that was just why I valued it. Tender she has been to me, and stern anon, as I have merited; but, would you understand the heart of woman, know if it be soft or hard, you will not trust her tenderness (or fear her sternness) to yourself; you will watch, with a prayer in your heart, for her tenderness to others.

She came late to our lunch that day, and explained that she had travelled by omnibus.

As she said the word omnibus, for some reason as yet mysterious to me, I saw the northern lights I love playing in the heaven of her face. I wondered why, but did not ask as yet, delaying, that I might watch those fairy fires of emotion, for her face was indeed like a star of which a little child told me the other day. I think some one must have told him first, for as we looked through the window one starlit night, he communicated very confidentially that whenever any one in the world shed a tear of pure pity, God's angels caught it in lily-cups and carried it right up to heaven, and that when God had thus collected enough of them, he made them into a new star. "So," said the little boy, "there must have been a good many kind people in the world to cry all those stars."

It was of that story I thought as I said to the Sphinx, —

"What is the matter, dear Madonna? Your face is the Star of Tears."

And then I ventured gently to tease her.

"What can have happened? No sooner did you speak the magic word 'omnibus,' than you were transfigured and taken from my sight in a silver cloud of tears. An omnibus does not usually awaken such tenderness, or call up northern lights to the face as one mentions it, . . . though," I added wistfully, "one has met passengers to and from heaven in its musty corners, travelled life's journey with them a penny stage, and lost them for ever. . . ."

"So," I further ventured, "may you have seemed to some fortunate fellow-passenger, an accidental companion of your wonder, as from your yellow throne by the driver . . ."

"Oh, do be quiet," she said, with a little flash of steel. "How can you be so flippant?" and then, noting the champagne, she exclaimed with fervor: "No wine for me to-day! It's heartless, it's brutal. All the world is heartless and brutal . . . how selfish we all are! Poor fellow! . . . I wish you could have seen his face!"

"I sincerely wish I could," I said, "for then I should no doubt have understood why the words 'omnibus' and 'champagne,' not unfamiliar words, should . . . well, make you look so beautiful."

"Oh, forgive me! Have n't I told you?"

she said, as absent-mindedly she watched the waiter filling her glass with champagne.

"Well," she continued, "you know the something Arms, where the 'bus always stops a minute or so on its way from Kensington. I was on top, near the driver, and, while we waited, my neighbour began to peel an orange and throw the pieces of peel down on to the pavement. Suddenly a dreadful, tattered figure of a man sprang out of some corner, and, eagerly picking up the pieces of peel, began ravenously to eat them, looking up hungrily for more. Poor fellow! he had quite a refined, gentle face, and I should n't have been surprised to hear him quote Horace, after the manner of Stevenson's gentlemen in distress. I was glad to see that the others noticed him too. Quite a murmur of sympathy sprang up amongst us, and a penny or two rang on the pavement. But it was the driver who did the thing that made me cry. He was one of those prosperous young drivers, with beaver hats and smart overcoats, and he had just lit a most well-to-do cigar. With the rest of us he had looked down on poor Lazarus, and for a moment, but only for a moment, with a certain contempt. Then a wonderful kindness came into his face, and, next minute, he had done a great deed — he had thrown Lazarus his newly-lit cigar."

"Splendid!" I ventured to interject.

"Yes, indeed!" she continued; "and I could n't help telling him so. . . . But you should have seen the poor fellow's face as he picked it up. Evidently his first thought was that it had fallen by mistake, and he made as if to return it to his patron. It was an impossible dream that it could be for him — a mere rancid cigar-end had been a windfall, but this was practically a complete, unsmoked cigar. But the driver nodded reassuringly, and then you should have seen the poor fellow's joy. There was almost a look of awe, that such fortune should have befallen him, and tears of gratitude sprang into his eyes. Really, I don't exaggerate a bit. I'd have given anything for you to have seen him — though it was heart-breaking, that terrible look of joy, such tragic joy. No look of misery or wretchedness could have touched one like that. Think how utterly, abjectly destitute one must be for a stranger's orange-peel to represent dessert, and an omnibus-driver's cigar set us crying for joy. . . ."

"Gentle heart," I said. "I fear poor Lazarus did not keep his cigar long. . . ."

"But why? . . ."

"Why? Is it not already among the stars, carried up by those angels who catch the tears of pity, and along with Uncle Toby's 'damn,' and such bric-à-brac, in God's museum of fair deeds? We shall see it shining down on us as the stars come out to-night. Yes! that will be a pretty astronomical theory to exchange with the little boy who told me that the stars are made of tears. Some are made of tears, I shall say, but some are the glowing ends of newly lit cigars, thrown down by good omnibus-drivers to poor, starving fellows who haven't a bed to sleep in, nor a dinner to eat, nor a heart to love them, and not even a single cigar left to put in their silver cigar-cases."

"That driver is sure of heaven, anyhow," said the Sphinx.

"Perhaps, dear, when the time comes for

us to arrive there, we will find him driving the station 'bus — who knows? But it was a pretty story, I must say. That driver deserves to be decorated."

"That's what I thought," said the Sphinx, eagerly.

"Yes! We might start a new society: *The League of Kind Hearts; a Society for the Encouragement of Acts of Kindness.* How would that do? Or we might endow a fund to bear the name of your 'bus-driver, and to be devoted in perpetuity to supplying destitute smokers with choice cigars."

"Yes," said the Sphinx, musingly, "that driver made me thoroughly ashamed of myself. I wish I was as sure of heaven as he is."

"But you *are* heaven," I whispered; "and *à propos* heaven, here is a little song which I wrote for you last night, and with which I propose presently to settle the bill. I call it the Silver Girl:

"'Whiter than whiteness was her breast,
　　And softer than new fallen snow,
So pure a peace, so deep a rest,
　　Yet purer peace below.

THE SILVER GIRL

"'Her face was like a moon-white flower
    That swayed upon an ivory stem,
Her hair a whispering silver shower,
    Each foot a silver gem.

"'And in a fair white house of dreams,
    With hallowed windows all of pearl,
She sat amid the haunted gleams,
    That little silver girl;

"'Sat singing songs of snowy white,
    And watched all day, with soft blue eyes,
Her white doves flying in her sight,
    And fed her butterflies.

"'Then when the long white day was passed,
    The white world sleeping in the moon,
White bed, and long white sleep at last —
    She will not waken soon.'"

WORDS WRITTEN TO MUSIC

It is one of the many advantages of that simplicity of taste which is ignorance, that an incorrigible incapacity for connoisseurship in the sister arts of cookery and music should enable one to be as happy with a bad dinner eaten to the sound of bad music, as others whose palates are attuned to the Neronian nightingales, and whose ears admit no harmonies less refined than the bejewelled harmonies of Chopin.

I have eaten dinners delicate as silverpoints, in rooms of canary-coloured quiet, where the candles burn hushedly in their little silken tents, and the soft voices of lovers rise and fall upon the dreaming ear; but I confess that it was the soothing quiet, the healing tones of light and colour, and the face of the Sphinx irradiated by some dream of halcyon's tongues *à la Persane*, rather than the beautiful food, that inspired my passionate peace. Mere roast lamb, new potatoes, and peas of living green had made me just as happy, gastronomically speaking, and I dare not mention what I order sometimes, and even day after day with a love that never tires, when I dine alone. Alone!

> . . . the very word is like a bell
> To toll me back from thee to my sole self;

for even this very night have I dined alone in a great solitude of social faces, low necks, electric lights, and the spirited band that has given me more pleasure than any music in London, always excepting my Bayreuth, the barrel-organ. Yes! strange as it may seem, I had come deliberately to hear this music, and secondarily to eat this dinner. What effect selections from Sullivan and "The Shop Girl," in collaboration with the three-and-sixpenny *table d'hôte*, would have upon more educated digestions it concerns me not to inquire; on mine they produce a sort of agonised ecstasy of loneliness — and to-night as I sat at our little lonely table in a corner of the great gallery and looked out across the glittering peristyle, ate that dinner and listened to that music, I shuddered with joy at my fearful loneliness.

I might have dined with the Beautiful, or have sent a telegraphic invitation to the Witty; I might have sat at meat with the Wise; but no! I would dine instead with the memories of dinners that were gone, and as the music did Miltonic battle near the ceiling, marched with clashing tread, or danced on myriad silken feet, wailed like the winds of the world, or laughed like the sun, my solitude grew peopled awhile with shapes fair and kind, who sat with me and lifted the glass and gave me their deep eyes, ladies who had intelligence in love, as Dante wrote, ladies of great gentleness and consolation, for whom God be thanked. But always in my ears, whatever the piece that was a-playing, the music came sweeping with dark surge across my fantasy, as though a sudden wind had dashed open a warm window, and let in a black night of homeless seas.

For in truth one I loved was out to-night on dark seas. She fares out across an ocean I have never sailed, to a land of which no man knows; and for her voyage she has only her silver feet, walking the inky waters, and the great light of her holy face to guide her steps. Ah! that I were with her to-night, walking hand in hand those dark waters. Oh, wherefore slip away thus companionless, fearless little voyager? Was it that I was unworthy to voyage those seas with you, that the weight of my mortality would have dragged down your bright immortality — youngest of the immortals. . . . From that sea which the Divine alone may tread, comes back no answer, nor light of any star; but there has stolen to my side and kissed my brow a shape dearer than all the rest, dear beyond dearness, a little earthly-heavenly shape who always comes when the rest have gone, and loves to find me sitting alone. She it is who leans her cheek against mine, as I try to read beautiful words out of the dead man's book at my side, she it is who whispers that we shall be too late to find a seat in the pit unless we hurry, and she it is who gaily takes my arm as we trot off together on happy feet. The great commissionaire takes no note of her, he thinks I am alone; besides we seldom go in hansoms, and seldom sit in stalls. . . . Enough, O Music! be merciful. Be lonely no more, lest you break the heart of the lonely.

"Ah! you have never seen her!" I whisper to myself as the waiter brings me my coffee —and I look at him again with a certain curiosity as I think that he has never seen her. Never to have seen her!

And then presently, as if in pity, the music will change; perhaps it will play some sustaining song of faith, and strike a sort of glory across one's heart, the haughty heart of sorrow; or it will be human and gay, and suddenly turn this solitude of diners into a sort of family gathering of humanity, throwing open sad hearts, that, like oneself, appear to be doing nothing but dine, and giving one glimpses into dreaming heads, linking, all in one great friendship of common joys and sorrows, the one sweet beginning, and the one mysterious end.

In this mood faces one has seen more than once become friends, and I confess that the sight of certain waiters moving in their accustomed places almost moved me to tears. Such is the pathos of familiarity.

So my thoughts took another turn, and I fell to thinking with tenderness of the friends about town that the Sphinx and I had made in our dinings — friends whom it had cost us but a few odd shillings and sixpences to make, yet friends we had fancied we might trust and even seek in a day of need. If they found me starving some night in the streets, I think they would take me in; and I think I know a coffee-stall man who would give me an early morning cup of coffee, and add a piece of cake, were I to come to him bare-footed some wintry dawn.

I have heard purists object to the smiles that are bought, as if smiles can or should be had for nothing, and as if it shows a bad nature in a waiter to smile more sweetly upon a shilling than a penny. After all, is he so far wrong in deeming the heart that prompts the shilling better worth a smile than the reluctant hand of copper? Besides, we are never so mean to ourselves as when we are mean to others. A few shillings per annum sown about town will surround the path of the diner with smiles year in and year out. The doors fly open as by magic at his approach, and the cosiest tables in a dozen restaurants are in perpetual reserve for him. I am even persuaded that a consistent generosity to cabmen gets known in due course among the fraternity, and that thus, in process of time, the nicest people may rely on getting the nicest hansoms — though this may be a dream. Certain I am that it brings luck to be kind to a pathetic race of men for whom I have a special tenderness, those amateur footmen, the cab-openers. Have you ever noticed the fine manners of some of them, and their lover-like gentleness with the silk skirts that it is theirs to save from soilure of muddy wheels? A practical head might reflect how much they do towards keeping down your wife's dressmaker's bills. I daresay they save her a dress a year — and yet they are not treated with gratitude as a race. How involuntarily one seems to assume that they will accept nothing over a penny, and how fingers, not penurious on other occasions, automatically reject silver as they ferret in pence-pockets for suitable alms! No! not alms — payment, and sometimes

WORDS WRITTEN TO MUSIC

poor payment, for a courtesy that adds another smile to your illusion of a smiling world.

Among the many lessons I have learnt from the Sphinx is one of the fair wage of the cab-opener. It was the very afternoon she had seen that cigar fall down from heaven, and her mood was thus the more attuned to pity. As we were about to drive away from the place of our lunching, having been ushered to our hansom by a tatterdemalion of distinguished manners, but marred unhappy countenance, I fumbled so long for the regulation twopence, that it seemed likely he should miss his reward or be run over, in running after it. But at that moment the Sphinx's hand shot past mine and dropped something into the outstretched palm. The man took it mechanically, but in a second his face flashed surprise. Evidently she had given him something extravagant. She was watching for his look, and telegraphed a smile that she meant it. Then you never saw such a figure of grateful joy as that shabby fellow became. His face fairly shone, and for a few moments he ran by our cabside wildly waving his hat, with an indescribable emotion of affectionate thankfulness.

"What did you give him, dear?" I asked.

"Never mind!"

"It was n't a sovereign?"

"Never mind!"

So I have never known what coin it was that thus transfigured him; but of this I am sure: that when the time of the great Terror has come to London, when the red flags wave on the barricades, and the puddles of red blood beneath the great guillotine in Trafalgar Square luridly catch the setting sun, the Sphinx and I will have a friend in that poor cab-opener.

There is another friend to whom we should fly for safety in those days of wrath. He, too, is a cab-opener, but, so to say, of higher rank — for he is the voluntary manager of a thriving cab-rank which we often have occasion to patronise. For some unknown reason he is always addressed as "Cap'n," and we never omit the courtesy as we salute him. So we have come to know him as the Captain of the Cab Rank. He is a short, thick-set, sturdy little man, with an overcoat buttoned straight beneath his chin, hands deep in his pockets, a firm, determined step, and a fiery face. He walks his pavement like a veritable captain on his quarter-deck, and his "Hansom up!" rings out like a stern word of command. At the call a shining door of the tavern opposite is thrown open with a slam, and a wild figure of a driver clatters across in terrified haste; with his head still wrapped in the warm glow he has just forsaken, he climbs his dark throne, and once more shakes the weary reins. Then as the little Captain briskly shuts us in, with a salute that seems to say that he has thus given us a successful start in life, and it is not his fault if we don't go on as we've begun, he blows a shrill note upon his whistle, half to call up the next cab to its place in the rank, half to signalise our departure, — as when sometimes a great boat sets out to sea they fire guns in the harbour, and excited crowds wave weeping handkerchiefs from the pier.

Yes! There are many faces I meet daily, faces I do business with and faces I take down to dinner, faces of the important and the brilliant, that I should miss much less than the little Captain of the Cab Rank. Our intercourse is of the slightest, we have little opportunities of studying each other's nature, and yet he is strangely vivid in my consciousness, quite a necessary figure in my picture of the world — so stamped is every part of him with that most appealing and attaching of all qualities, that of our common human nature. He has the great gift of character, and however poor and humble his lot, failure is surely no word to describe him, for he is a personality, and to be a personality is to have succeeded in life.

Yes! I often think of the Captain as I think of the famous characters in fiction, or notable figures in history; and I should feel very proud if I could believe he sometimes thought of me.

Well, well . . . it is late. The bill, waiter, please! Good-night! Good-night!

AT ELIM ARE TWELVE WELLS

WE are told that sorcery and divination are once more living spiritual methods amongst us — that witches' Sabbaths are held in Paris, and that the philosopher's stone is being sought in London. It is likely enough, and indeed it has never been unlikely, for in so mysterious a world one never knows by what method we may hit the truth, and it is wisest to try all — from divining-rod to scalpel. However, it is a subject in which I am but generally interested, as one of the great body of the superstitious, and my personal experiments are confined to a very innocent form of divination — the ancient divination by books. Virgil and the Bible used to be the books mainly favoured by old consultants of the "sortes," and the Bible, by its long sacred associations, remains, of course, the most impressive book to consult, if you would take the oracle more or less seriously. I am given to the practice trivially with all my books — have indeed sought to learn my fate from a book by Mr. Jerome, or a volume of essays by Mr. Andrew Lang. Calendars with texts or quotations from poets have no inconsiderable influence upon my life, and often, on rising, I consult my Shakspere almanac with no little anxiety. But, I suppose, it is the Puritan fathers in my blood that send me most often, and when I mean it most, to the Bible.

This morning, rising, for no reason that I know of, in the worst of spirits, and looking gloomily out across an expanse of sunlit gorse and heather that should have gladdened any grateful soul, indifferent to the lark and spiteful towards the cuckoo, I took a Bible down from my shelf of bed-books, and, opening it at random, read: *At Elim are twelve wells and seventy palm-trees!* From that instant, no doubt illogically enough, my spirits began to lift, and all through the day, whenever they momentarily fell again, as some dark or wistful thought gloomed or wailed through my mind, " Never mind! " the sweet old words kept whispering, "at Elim are twelve wells and seventy palm-trees! "

TWELVE WELLS

When the children of Israel had exhausted the first excitement of crossing the Red Sea, when the intoxication of their triumph was failing them, and the song of Moses and the timbrel of Miriam were no longer in their ears, they began to murmur for water, but found only the waters of Marah. Then, as Moses sweetened the waters with the green boughs, and reproved their discontent, he told them of Elim, a pleasant place but a day's march or so away; and as they fared on wearily through that desert of Shur, how often must they have said to each other: *At Elim are twelve wells and seventy palm-trees* — the very words full of cool water and cool shade.

For all I know, the wells of Elim are long since dry, its palm-trees withered, its very name forgotten; and to us of another age and civilisation the very symbolism is unfamiliar, we who go not to wells for our water, and have never seen a palm-tree. Yet such is the emotional impressionability of words, such their power of transmitting sincerity of feeling across time, that those simple words of cool water and cool shade vibrate still with their old exquisite refreshment of promise; still speak, like spring water in the eager mouth, of quenched thirst and the whisper of leaves; still make a mirage to the mind of the mysterious mossy walls of old wells, the delicious plash and echo, the sleepy sunlight stealing on tip-toe through the tendrilled patterned shade, to kiss with sudden glory some little darkling fern,— quenched thirst, and all the great green rest.

Yes; great is the comfort of words — really there is no comfort save in words. It is not in what the words say — not in what they tell or promise or counsel us. For the most comforting words are often the most irrelevant — particularly as the mood for which we seek their aid is usually one of vague melancholy and undefined distress, mere spiritual *ennui* and weariness of the soul. No! it is something in the fall of the syllables, in the flower-like face of the words; perhaps it is the tranquillising presence of perfection, a sense of that eternity which lives in all beauty. Here is something complete to calm the ache of our incompleteness, here is something at peace with itself, here is something that has found the perfect rest of the perfect.

TWELVE WELLS

In fact, curiously, the words which thus comfort us most are often the saddest — broken cries of ancient heart-break, wistful calls of long stilled passion, petals from the rose of old beauty, and poignant phrases of the passing of the world.

"I loved thee, Atthis, long ago," cried Sappho, and time has but deepened the yearning of that old regret. Yet the sigh that tore her heart, by some curious alchemy, brings a strange comfort to ours, that alchemy of time that turns old tears to pearls, and old mirth to melancholy — and so we go happy-sad a summer-day for the ghostly echo of that old anguished cry.

Sic transit gloria mundi! Familiar and even vulgarised as are the words, what a noble chord they still strike in the heart, the mighty Latin clothing the passing of the world in such pomp of imperial phrase as almost to suggest, even while it writes this epitaph of an universe, that somehow the glory can never pass away, throwing over its mortality the purple pall of a hinted immortality.

The pathos of the Greek Anthology, the

haunting cadences of Omar Khayyam, sad old refrains from Theocritus — it is such expressions of old passion, pessimism, and despair that, strangely enough, most comfort the heart. Strange that the twelfth chapter of Ecclesiastes should bring so keen a delight, and the sorrows of Job become a joy for ever!

Thus it was that the twelve wells and seventy palm-trees of a long-lost Elim came to comfort me this morning. So have we all been comforted by the sudden song of a bird heard in a fortunate moment, or by sudden sunlight on a rose; by a thousand inspiring surprises of sight and sound which promised nothing beyond the joy of their accident.

It is not that I believe in Elim that Elim comforts me; but because the old writer, by the simple sincerity of his art, has made in those nine simple words a picture of rest that is an Elim in itself. In the very words themselves, are there not twelve wells and seventy palm-trees?

THE BLUE JAR

RECENTLY I was invited to hear music in the house of a rich man. It was a great house and gorgeous, and yet not without a certain taste in its furnishing and its decoration, a taste uncharacteristic, uncommitting, and indeed representative, somewhat incongruously, of the various tastes of the many poor artists who had built and beautified it, rather than of any vivifying taste in the one rich man who occasionally occupied it.

"How beautiful we artists make the world — for others!" I sighed, as my soul went out to the enslaved architects and painters and artificers, famous, unknown, or infamous, who had breathed their fatal passion for beauty into this rich man's marbles, woven it into his tapestries, dyed with their hearts' blood his coloured glass, given their dreams into his bondage, and put their very souls beneath his feet. Sad artists who in every corner of this house had worked with tears!

And here were the musicians! Music too was a slave in this house. The bondsmen came with their long hair and white faces, carrying their captive instruments in their hands, the deep-lunged violoncello that breaks the heart, and the little violin that brings the tears. And with them too they carried in little cages of manuscript the singing souls of the great composers of old time, whom to-night they would re-embody — they would open the dark manuscripts and the souls would fly forth among the strings — re-embody — that Beethoven might once more utter his soul's agony, and the rich man's evening thus pass pleasantly by.

There were many women seated in the hall, some beautiful; they wore many garments of great costliness, some beautiful; and upon their necks and in their hair glittered many jewels, some beautiful. But I noted that the fairest jewels were upon the necks least fair — yet maybe kindly so, for thus were they not upon the necks that most needed them?

"Yes," but in that fantastic mood which music induces, I pursued the question a step further: "Have the beautiful stones them-

THE BLUE JAR

selves no feelings, no preferences? How can those diamonds glitter so in that terrible old lady's hair? And are those pearls really happy round yonder yellow neck? They used to live once rocking and shimmering deep down in a wonderful ocean. . . "

And as I mused, methought the pearls answered:—

"We pearls are never happy," they said, "but there is a neck seated next to you where indeed it would be a joy to live; . . . " and a great tear stole down from the necklet and fell into the lap of its mistress, who caught it and remarked to her neighbour that one of her pearls had been trying to escape.

There seems to me a certain indecency, even immorality, in performing great music to so trivial and commonplace a company of men and women as that among which I was seated. It is, of course, but a part of the general profanation of the holy arts by the vulgar, a profanation, however, in which perhaps music suffers most, from the intense intimacy of its noblest and most attractive inspirations. Architecture for the most part shields itself by building ugly buildings for most possible purposes, but even when it builds beautifully for base uses, it is not, after all, a sensitive personal art, and though the soul of the architect passing by and beholding the money changers in his beautiful halls cannot but suffer, the marble is not so acutely himself as the notes of a requiem or the words of a lyric are the very flesh of the composer or the poet. The painter too may hide his soul away behind some impersonal subject, or in some corner of a picture where few eyes are likely to seek it. The poet escapes through the sheer indifference of the vulgar. Great poetry is of no use to amuse a crowd, nor will it soothe the savage breast of the diner, as he sits ruddy at evening, with napkin hanging from his neck and his champagne laughing at his side. Poetry has to be read to be understood — music needs only to be played.

But music, like Latin or Greek, has an aural decorative quality, a patterned surface of amusing sound, accidental to its serious messages of joy and sorrow. It is autobiography suitable for framing — it is a tragic utterance of the human soul which you may use as you use tortoise-shell, without a thought

THE BLUE JAR

of the tortoise. Music is a beautiful woman singing in an unknown tongue — some few love what she sings, but most see only one more woman to desire.

It has been suggested that the favourite music of the gods is the picturesque murmur of human agony, as, deprived by distance of intelligible and responsible meaning, it mounts on high, just as the desperate buzzings of imprisoned and bewildered insects actually full of pain, strike rich chords of frenzy and humorous rage to the ear of man. Play us the Crucifixion! "*Eloi Eloi, lama sabacthani*" — what exquisite anguish is there! And it is in some such mood of purely æsthetic detachment that we listen to the music of the great German and Italian masters. The swan is dying, in great agony of spirit — but alas! for our pity, it is dying so beautifully! It is singing so wonderful a song!

"Adelaïda! Adelaïda!" cries Beethoven, and his heart breaks in the cry — ah! but the cry is so beautiful! Go on breaking for ever, great heart of music, so that sometimes after dinner, we may hear again that beautiful cry!

"Adelaïda!"

I had not noticed that among the musicians had been brought in a wonderful captive woman, very tall and lovely, and regally simple. It was she who was singing. She was like a Greek temple to look on, faultlessly built of white marble; or like some moonlit tower of Italy which sways like a lily from afar.

There was in that great hall but one other thing as beautiful as she, — a little jar of unfathomable blue, with smooth simple sides, which at the same moment I caught sight of, cloistered and calm in a niche high above us: simple in shape as a maid, simple in colour as a violet, and all mysterious as a star.

At last the evening had succeeded. Down upon our troubled sea of incongruities, upon mediocrity absurdly arrayed as magnificence, upon pretentious plainness foolish with gems, down upon the idle chatter and cheat of it all shone the steady unflinching blue of that little blue jar. Here at last was something sufficient, complete, elemental, eternal. I know nothing of pottery, and I knew as little of the history of my jar as of the beautiful Greek Temple who was singing. It was but

THE BLUE JAR

two curves, like the neck and the breast of a girl, enclosing a whole heaven of blue. But it was perfect, perfect with the simplicity of eternal things. It was complete in perfection as a great line of poetry, as the flight of a bird, as the curve of a falling wave. It was all.

From that night I remember no woman's face, no splendid lady, no single particular of all that lavish magnificence.

I remember only that little blue jar.

A DANISH BATHING-PLACE

SAND, sea, and sky are, I suppose, sand, sea, and sky all the world over. Yet there are, doubtless, places where the sand is cleaner, harder, and more spacious, the sea greener and fresher, and where the sky at all events looks more boundless. Such a place, we may say, is not Lancashire Southport, where the sand is so dirty that the dainty sea seldom does more than visit the horizon verge; it is not fashionable and over-rated Cromer, with its untidy mud cliffs ever tumbling down into unsightly chaos; but it emphatically is Fanö, a Danish island, stretching itself for some seventeen miles along the North Sea, on a line say with Edinburgh. Island it is called, but rather is it a huge silver sandbank, seventeen miles long, and at its broadest point two miles broad, of low sandhills grown over with a sort of sea-wheat. It has one little port,

A DANISH BATHING-PLACE

Nordby, on the inland side, where you reach it from Liverpool Street viâ Harwich and Esbjerg, a red hotel and a cluster of quaint houses, making a picturesque landing-place. But here is not your stay. Here you but land to drive the mile and a half across the island, finally to emerge on three big hotels and a few pretty villas, keeping more or less together in a vast and sandy loneliness, which suddenly opens like a thousand doors on to the sea.

I am but little of an Odysseus, so I shall not venture to assert that the air you now breathe is the purest, the sand the cleanest and most exquisite to the tread, the most grateful to the eye, the sea-line the most delightful bathing-place in the whole world. I have a timid idea that the world is a big place; but this I will venture to say, that for sand, sea, and sky at their best Fanö must prove hard to beat. There is certainly no English watering-place known to me that can compare with it in all those respects for which we go down to the seaside in flannels; and in this I am confirmed by an English family, the only English family that so far has discovered Fanö, — a discovery which its more charming members have gone on keeping to themselves for eleven successive years. At length, however, they feel that, as the Theosophist would say, the time has come for Fanö to be revealed to the world, and it is, therefore, not without consulting their security, that I make this communication. Indeed, though some of them have mastered the beautiful Danish tongue in the course of their visits, they have grown to feel that a few more English voices would improve the sound of table d'hôte.

Personally, I confess that one of the most original charms of Fanö for me is that it provides also so complete a holiday from speech. Being fortunately unable to speak German, and knowing as much of Danish as I do of Persian, I was able to live in an enchanted palace of silence, in which only one kind voice could reach me; to be invulnerable to speech, and yet alive to all the charm of sound — for words are so beautiful so long as we don't know their meaning. I love the society of my fellows so long as I cannot understand what they say. Foreigners always seem so wonderful to me just on that account. Thus I rather revelled in my solitude of Danes and Germans, and loved to sit, as it were, invisible amongst them, while the brilliant Danish flashed and sighed from lip to lip.

> Danes, charming Danes,
> I know not what you mean!

There was one Danish gentleman I found that I could talk a little to, Pyramus and Thisbe-like, through little broken chinks in the wall of silence, and our talk was so pleasant that I repented for a moment my Trappist vow. For we talked of literature, and it is so seldom one meets an Englishman one can talk literature with. Every Dane, on the contrary, was once a literary man in his youth. My acquaintance was, I gathered, a business man, but then our very hotel-keeper had been a student at the University, and was a disciple of George Brandes! Denmark reminded me of Scotland in that. How many business men in England, I wonder, could talk as intelligently of English literature as that Dane talked that evening — of what one must remember is to him a foreign literature? Outside, a nation's literature seems so much — inside, how little! England is Shakspere and Byron and Dickens only to the foreigners — Denmark is Hans Andersen and Brandes to itself, as Scotland is Burns.

My friend asked a question which quaintly illustrated how much more our literature is to other nations than it is to ourselves. Near us was a bright little English boy, everyone's playfellow, named Percy. "Percy?" asked my Danish friend. "Is he called so after your poet Shelley?" I had to assure him that English boys were not as a rule named after the English poets, and that the prevalence of the name John was not to be taken as evidence of the popularity of Keats.

Fanö does not aim at excitement. It gives you rest. On the endless yellow shore there are bathing-vans, bicycles, and those great hooded wicker-chairs one associates with Trouville. The firm platform-like expanse of sand makes it particularly delightful for bicycling, and to bicycle by the sea is to feel like a disembodied spirit. I found it, too, very good sand to sit and do nothing on.

A DANISH BATHING-PLACE

Up at the Kur Hotel there is a band which plays some time before you are up, and again in the evening. Then there are quaint little "balls" sometimes at the Kur Hotel, in which the peasants in their curious, mournful costumes, are to be seen taking a part. There is likewise a tennis-lawn, and, during our stay, a kind German gentleman let off a small quantity of rockets. We had, too, one of the most picturesque night thunderstorms I ever remember. But, on the whole, I repeat, Fanö does not aim at excitement. It brings you rest.

The cooking? Well, hotel cuisine is the favourite subject of a greater pen than mine. I was assured by one gentleman that Danish cooking is the finest cooking in the world. "Oh, I don't know," I ventured to reply, "they cook very well in Afghanistan." He had n't been there, he said, so I thought he might have modified his statement. But, of course, Danish cooking is famous, and deservedly so. There are many Danish dishes which we might well add to our menu.

And about the fish there cannot be two opinions. Fish so exquisitely fresh *cannot* be had in England, for the reason that fish in Denmark are sold alive. The fish-shops are great tanks, in which the fish go on swimming till they attract a customer. The fish, therefore, always came to our hotel alive, — a method which prolongs life, and much improves the taste of the fish after death.

AN AFFECTIONATE LETTER FROM TABBY

Young Sebastian, who is just standing on the dewy threshold of a brilliant literary reputation, called on me the other day, happy as a girl. He is as yet innocent of the dark underground passages beneath the Temple of Fame, and has not yet heard the fearful shriek of some young reputation as it is carried away by the cat-like priests to torture, and perchance death, in those horrid vaults.

"I've just had such a delightful letter from —— " he said, naming a certain distinguished majordomo of letters, whose success is not perhaps so entirely unconnected with literary arts as his enemies would say.

"Why, you grow pale," he said, "the tears start to your eyes!"

"Yes! I grow pale for you," I said; "so Tabby is already in your path."

"What do you mean?" he said. "Surely —— is an important critic, and I don't think I ever received a kinder letter in my life."

"Of that I haven't the smallest doubt," I answered. "For I too have had affectionate letters from Tabby — and my tears start to think of the boyishness of heart with which, just like you, I rejoiced in them. Yes, in the fulness of my guileless youth I once opened my heart to Tabby. I was so grateful to him that I even thought I admired his poetry. That is five years ago, and Tabby and I write no more loving letters to each other. . . ."

"It only means, I suppose, that you have quarrelled," Sebastian interrupted impatiently.

"Unhappy boy," I proceeded calmly, "shall I be able to save you from Tabby? At all events, however it wrings your young heart, and however angry you get, I must try. I know it is hard, poor boy. You are so much in love with his praise. But it must be done."

With that I rose, and, unlocking a drawer of my desk, drew forth a packet of letters with a sigh. Along with the letters was a smaller packet of newspaper cuttings.

"Before you show me your letter, you shall

LETTER FROM TABBY

read one of mine," I said. "I could not bear to read them all again. It would too painfully remind me of the days for ever gone when Tabby used to ask me to meet General . . ."

"General ——" suggested Sebastian.

"Ah! has he asked you to meet him already? How simple great military men are! I believe he feels it quite an honour to be asked to meet Tabby's latest minor poet."

"Well, here is one that will do," I continued, selecting a prettily-written letter of eight pages. "Read this."

As Sebastian read his face grew perplexed, and as he finished it was full of disappointment.

"Why!" he said, "it's almost the same letter as mine, with a slight difference in the wording."

"Ah!" I said. "Well! now read this. You have seen what the letter says about my 'New Poems'; now read this article."

The article was a bitterly contemptuous piece of work charged with subtle depreciation.

"You don't mean to say that he wrote that?" Sebastian exclaimed.

"I know he did," I answered.

"But it's not possible. There must be some mistake. The man who would do that must be the meanest thing that crawls. . . ."

"That's Tabby," I replied.

It was Sebastian's turn to grow pale, and angry tears of disappointment were not far from his clear young eyes.

"I'm so sorry for you," I said. "I won't show you any more of them, though for each of these pretty letters I could show you a poisoned paragraph, or a cloaked assassin of a review. It is Tabby's way — that's why we call him Tabby — that is, velvet and claws. Here in one packet is the velvet, here in the other are the claws. You can hardly call him an enemy, because, though he looks and dresses like a man, he has the mind of a maiden aunt, bitter with disappointment and edged with gossip."

"Can it really be true?" poor Sebastian moaned.

"It is all too true, my poor Sebastian; and I have still a stranger thing to tell you about Tabby. It is perhaps the reason of his being Tabby. *He is not really a living man.* You

LETTER FROM TABBY

start? But it is quite true. Some ten years ago when poor Tabby was beginning to sport himself in the literary beam, a certain great critic swept down on Tabby and killed him. It was a little cruel, perhaps; but the horrible thing about it all was that Tabby did not honestly die, but began life again as a vampire. Tabby is dead, though he still presides at literary functions and makes polished addresses, quite dead; but the dangerous thing about him is that he is of *the dead who scratch*. Tabby, I say, lives mainly on his practice as a vampire. Whenever he sees a young reputation stepping gaily along the road of literary fame, he sidles up to it with charming manners and intoxicating praise. Then he sucks the blood of its young confidence, and by various devilish arts, not good for us even to imagine, draws the life from the poor young thing — till some day it finds its strength failing it — it is fading away, and the last cause it suspects is — Tabby."

"But why should he follow so horrible a calling?" asked Sebastian.

"He fears the young, and yet it is only by killing and feeding on the young that he can keep up his semblance of life. The moment a young reputation escapes him his end is near."

"His end *is* near," answered Sebastian, and as I looked at his stern young face, a weak twinge of ancient affection prompted a momentary pity for Tabby. Tabby will suffer so as he dies.

DESIDERIUM

I THOUGHT that my mother came to me and said: "Child, you have forgotten me."

And I answered: "But I have not forgotten Her."

And my sister came to me and said: "Brother, you have forgotten me."

And I answered: "But I have not forgotten Her."

Then came the friend of my heart, and he said: "Where is our love?"

And I said: "It is with Her."

Then I thought my youth came, holy, with sad eyes, and said: "Where are our dreams?"

And I answered: "O, tell me where is She?"

Then came the Earth and the Heaven. And the Earth said: "Have you forgotten those mornings in the dew, when you lay on my green bosom and loved every little blade of the grass that grows there?"

"No," I answered, "I have not forgotten, for is not your bosom greener because of Her?"

And Heaven said: "You have forgotten — forgotten those pure nights when against the cold cheek of the moon you laid the throbbing face of your boyhood, and kissed with your young lips each of my little stars."

"No," I said, "I have not forgotten — for I loved you because of Her."

And a woman came, and said: "You will forget me."

And I answered : "Never — until I meet Her."

THE SECOND COMING OF THE IDEAL

ONE Sunday morning, a few months ago, I passed along the sumptuous corridors of the Waldorf-Astoria Hotel, New York, on my way to the writing-room, and I came to a spacious scarlet hall, set about with plush couches and little writing-desks. Exquisite and imperious women sat in cosy flirtation with respectful young Americans, and there was a happy buzz of vanity in the air. Wealth, luxury, idleness, were all about me, purring and sunning themselves in the electric light; and yet, for some unknown and doubtless trivial reason, I was sad. As I look back I can only account for my sadness by the fact that I was to sit answering week-old letters, while these happy people flirted. A little reason is always the best to give for a great sadness — though, indeed, how could one help being sad in the presence of so much marble and so many millionaires!

Well, at all events I was sad; but suddenly, as I looked about for an unoccupied desk, what was this voice of ancient comfort speaking to me from a little group, one reader and two listeners, — a grey-haired, rather stern, old man, a grey-haired old lady, a boy, not specially intent, — rich people, you would say, to look at them: "*Many waters cannot quench love, neither can the floods drown it; if a man would give all the substance of his house for love it would utterly be contemned.*"

It was a New England father persisting in a private morning service here among the triflers.

I felt like those of whom one has read in Sunday-school stories, who, passing the door of some little mission-house one rainy night, heard a word or a hymn that seemed miraculously intended for them. Surely that stern old Puritan father had been led to read that particular chapter, that particular Sunday morning, more for my sake than, at all events, for the sake of his little boy, who might quite reasonably and respectfully have complained that he was too young as yet to comprehend writing so profoundly beautiful and suggestive as the Hebrew scriptures.

Yes! it was evidently for the poor idealist in the House of Astor that the message was intended. For the boy weariness, for the mother platitude, for the father a text — for me a bird singing; and all day long I kept saying to myself, lonely there among the millionaires: "*Many waters shall not quench love, neither shall the floods drown it; if a man would give all the substance of his house for love, it would utterly be contemned.*"

If a wild rose had suddenly showered its petals down from the ceiling, or a spring bubbled up through the floor, or a dove passed in flight through the hall, the effect of contrast could hardly have been more unexpected than the surprising sound of those old words thus spoken at that moment, in that place. They had for the ear the same shock of incongruity, of wilful transportation out of one world into another quite alien, which Cleopatra's Needle has for the eye amid the hansoms and railway-bridges of the Thames' embankment, or the still greater shock of juxtaposition with which one looks upon the Egytian obelisk in Central Park.

But there was this difference. The obelisks tell of a dead greatness, of a power passed away, whereas those words told of an ever-living truth, and bore witness, even by their very quotation in such a context, to a power no materialism can crush, no pessimism stifle, the deathless idealism of the human spirit.

That the heart of man can still go on dreaming after all these centuries of pain and superficial disillusion is perhaps the greatest proof of the authenticity of his dreams. How often, indeed, must such words, such promises of the poet and the prophet, have rung as with a hollow mockery in the ears of man; in the downfall of despairing peoples, with all their unregarded débris of individual hopes and dreams; in dark ages of oppression, iron epochs of militarism in which the very flowers might well have feared to blossom, the very birds to sing; and in the ears of no people so hopelessly as of that whose poet gave us this song of songs; that people which, as if in ironical return for the persecution of ages, has contributed most to the idealism of mankind. Yet, through all, the indomitable dreams arise, and

IDEALISM

the indestructible words promise on as of old. Though the dream passes into the dust, the dust rises again in the dream.

But idealism has deadlier foes than the iron heel of the soldier, or the rack of the priest — each in his way sometimes a stern idealist himself; it has even more to fear from the slothful materialism of luxury, the sneer of cynicism, and those fashions of philosophy which hold up the dust in derision of the dream. Being an eternal principle in Nature, idealism has nothing to fear from any, or all, of the three. It cannot die — it can only

> "Suffer a sea-change
> Into something rich and strange."

It may be darkened during more or less lengthy periods of eclipse, but from all such periods it has come out brighter than ever before, and it is perhaps from the most serious period of eclipse in its history that I hold it to be at present emerging.

Of course, it must not be forgotten that in the darkest of such periods, the area of eclipse has always been relative, and has never covered the whole or even the majority of mankind. As literature and art are our only, or our chief, means of making an estimate, perhaps we lay undue stress on their changing temper from time to time, and too easily grant the implied presumption of a few specialized individuals to speak for the world at large. As in political elections there is always a large proportion of non-voters, including perhaps a majority of wise heads; so in this matter of spiritual representation there are comparatively few who record their votes. And it may well be that these silent ponderers on the mystery of life are the best worth hearing.

It is in the nature of heresies to make a noise, and doubt and dissatisfaction always gain an advertisement out of all proportion to their representative value. Whatever doubts and fears have darkened the souls of philosophers during the last nineteen hundred years, however bitterly or drearily or tragically they have read the riddle of life, we must not forget that there have been Christians all the time, — Christians quite content with their own answer to the

IDEALISM

riddle; as, indeed (to refer to a still more complete and apparently final, eclipse) throughout the Christian era, there have been worshippers of the old gods all the time; and as also, in the vicissitudes of both, and ages before either were thought of, there has been the Hebrew, equally contented with his answer to the riddle all the time. Similarly, to compare small things with great, amid all the mirk of French realism, men have gone on quietly enjoying Jane Austen and Sir Walter all the time.

Perhaps, indeed, while it has been the most superficially sensitive, it has not been the profoundest amongst us, or at all events a majority of the profound, who have been most conscious of the recent eclipse of idealism; and yet it were idle to deny that many profound and serious minds have, during the last twenty years or so, come under its shadow.

To some, indeed, in religion, in politics, in literature and all the arts, idealism has seemed to go down for ever before a criticism which has called itself realism, but which, when it has not been mere superficialism, has really been one of the friends of idealism in disguise. In religion, despair; in politics, selfishness; in literature and all the arts, the hard and ugly and cynical surface. And perhaps, in the field of politics this is hardly the hour to make an annunciation of the ideal. Think of Armenia! Think of Dreyfus!

In fact, idealism in politics seems for the moment to have forsaken Europe to take refuge with those American arms which have made themselves the unselfish champions of an oppressed people; though, alas! when we turn from the idealism of American foreign politics to enquire concerning the progress of democracy in the greatest democratic nation in the world, we may well pause in our optimism and await developments.

Thirty or forty years ago it seemed indeed as if the world were at last to have an opportunity of being governed on some broader principle than narrow commercial interests, and that at last the application of moral ideas to politics was to be attempted. Such was the illusion created by the eloquence of John Bright and Mr. Gladstone, and the moral enthusiasm of Mr. John Morley. Much later, we dreamed a brief dream of a like beautiful rose-colour during the phantom morning of Lord Roseberry's short and merry administration. But alas! the cynic and the diplomatist and the usurer once more pull the strings of nations, and Toryism, bloody and unabashed, again lifts its head in the counsels of the world.

Certainly if in politics the present hour is not that darkest hour that precedes the dawn, we may well despair.

But the dawn necessarily comes latest in politics; and perhaps the mission of the successful politician is rather to fight than to announce the dawn.

However, turning to fields from which the news is more momentous to the human soul, and applying to such watchmen of morning as the poet, the artist, and the philosopher, the news is more cheering — though for the past twenty years it has been cheerless enough.

No doubt man is a good deal of a coward, and a very little alarm will make him cry out that all is lost. Rob him of his trinity, and he cries out that you have stolen his religion;

frighten away his dryads and his fauns, his ribboned shepherds and shepherdesses, and with Keats, he declares that "beauty and loveliness have passed away." Run a railway through the Lake District and Mr. Ruskin conceives that the world is no longer beautiful. For man's hold on the realities is so uncertain that they have only to change the fashion of their garments for him to believe them lost for ever. In any new form he finds an enemy of some old faith — instead of the friend it probably is. He seems incapable of learning that the gods are always changing their names.

Most of man's troubles, many of his tragedies, and perhaps all his despairs, have sprung and still spring from the simple fact of his being so incorrigible a formalist.

There is nothing man loves so much as to make laws that he knows he cannot live up to; to immolate himself on impossible altars; to take two words that really mean the same thing, and shed his blood for them. And, indeed, there is seldom a battle in which both sides are not fighting for the same cause.

IDEALISM

Will man never learn to apply to his own generation that old text which proclaims that "the letter killeth, but the spirit giveth life"? It was for this sin that idealism has died, over and over again. It is for this sin, too, that realism is dying. Will idealism, one wonders, be any wiser now that it is so surely being born again?

What do I mean by idealism? I use the word in no technically philosophical or narrowly artistic sense. I mean by idealism, the attitude of those who insist on the beautiful in human life, and consider that the beautiful rather than the ugly contains the key to its mysterious meaning. In short, one might say that idealism is man's optimistic deduction from the beautiful; or still more briefly, that idealism is the optimism of the beautiful, as so-called "realism" has been the pessimism of the ugly. The favorite moods of idealism are love and wonder, of realism scrutiny and scepticism. The idealist is a poet, the realist is his critic. Realism, properly understood, is only one of the methods of idealism, and it is its work, by breaking up the old forms into which idealism from time to time hardens, to prepare the world for new expressions of the ideal.

That the heart of idealism has failed it, is no doubt due, even in its most indirect manifestations of lost courage, to the destructive theological criticism brought to bear on religion by the physical sciences on the one hand and literary criticism on the other. That the Bible may be fallible as history and symbolic as revelation, is in the end nothing against its supreme authority as the Book of the Soul. The childish cosmogony and the legendary history of the Iliad of the Hebrews detract nothing from its matchless spiritual science. Jonah is no relevant argument against St. John.

Already even the time is past when speculative curates could make a fashionable reputation for engaging heterodoxy on the quaintnesses of antique faith, and that idealism should ever have been alarmed by the easily-won victories of secularism marks what would appear to be one of the eternal weaknesses of its constitution.

For the worst of idealism is that it is always giving the wrong reasons for itself.

IDEALISM 75

Instead of courageously taking its stand on its own intrinsic certitude, on the facts of its great feelings, on the evidences for itself in the deep heart of human nature, it clings to documents, to the superseded expressions of old moods of inspiration and moments of insight. It quotes past authority, instead of present perception, and thus realism, which is merely another name for science, explodes the authority, and for a while idealism is disconsolate.

For example, idealism began long ago with the belief that man was what we call a spiritual being, and in proof thereof pointed to such well-known facts of man's supremacy as the acknowledged fact that sun, moon, and stars revolved round the world! But when Copernicus came and declared this bad astronomy, idealism took fright, and for a while feared that man might not be a spirit, after all. Yet it had only given a bad reason for a good belief. And this one may take as typical of the kind of mistakes idealism has all along been making and realism correcting.

By a spiritual being one is driven to the

conclusion that one really means a being eternally individual and responsible; a being whose dreams are not limited by life, and whose duties are not ended by death. The present writer in an earlier stage of his development somewhat too lightly called in question the present value of the concept of the hereafter of the soul, the immortal continuity of the individual. Its tendency, he once feared, was to minimise the significance of our present existence. He now sees — or thinks he sees — that the precise opposite is the truth, and that not only is the significance of a man's life intensified by, but perhaps, indeed, it entirely depends upon, its enduring for ever.

We have often been told, and perhaps have ourselves often declared it, that this desire for immortality, this pathetic longing for continued existence, is merely the lust of egoism, a deceit of full blood; and a great poet has thanked " whatever gods there be " —

> " That no life lives for ever,
> That dead men rise up never,
> That even the weariest river
> Winds somewhere safe to sea."

IDEALISM

But to be tired of the disappointments of life is not to be tired of life, and perhaps the lover is wiser, who amid all the uncertainties and frustrations and agonies of love, hopes only for one final satisfaction, and in that hope alone is content, its eternal continuance. No true lover is satisfied without a promise, or at least a hope, that the love for a year or a day will develop into the love that lasts alway.

> He "cannot be at peace
> In having love upon a mortal lease."

In spite of the reason which tells us that beauty is beauty, and delight delight, for however short a time we hold it in our hands, its lasting for ever seems to be a condition of completeness in any human enterprise or interest worth beginning. The love that cannot last for ever should take some other name.

Indirectly the whole of mortal aspiration rests upon man's instinctive, mostly unconscious, reliance that it is for some divine immortal end. No morality will be strong enough ultimately to take the place of immortal responsibility as an incentive, though for a time, to use a homely image, morality, like a train from which the locomotive has been detached while still in motion, will appear to move of itself, from the momentum of old religion. There will be good socialists for a while because of the Christian altruism stored in their blood; but it cannot be long before those who have transferred their egos to the state, and exchanged their own personal hopes of salvation for an abstract hope of the good of the race, will be asking themselves why a race doomed to perish is any more important in kind than an individual similarly doomed. Either the individual is everything — or the race is nothing. Either man is a spirit, that is, a being whose actions and destinies have an eternal significance, or the world is a preposterous masquerade, worth taking part in for those who can light-heartedly repose in the movement and colour of it, but hardly worth the pain of a toothache, and certainly quite unworthy the cost of a single martyrdom.

It is the way of man first to dream, then to doubt, then to despair, and finally to sneer both at his dream, his doubt, and his despair.

IDEALISM

Human history is continually going this round of evolution — with its poets, its sceptics, its pessimists, and its cynics. An age of spiritual despair has recently passed into a brief period of bitter and brutal cynicism, but the moon of change is once more bringing in the dreams. Once more man begins to "think nobly of the soul." Certain coarse old voices will no doubt have him merely a ridiculous animal still, but their audiences are thinning. Young men, in belated imitation, are to be heard preaching their little gospels of brutality, and vainly hoping to stem the rising tide of idealism by miscalling it "sentimentalism," but such are wearing last year's fashions. There has never been sufficient life in cynicism to allow it a long day. A little stinging fly, it loses its sting as it uses it — and though the natural history of the illustration be fabulous, its application will serve. Sentimentalism! After all, is there any sentimentalism more shallow and dangerous than the sentimentalism of brute force, the sentimentalism which glorifies man's lust of destruction, and bids the ape and the tiger rise again? If to practise pity, and to seek peace be sentimentalism, to prefer gentleness to cruelty, beauty to ugliness, self-sacrifice to selfishness, — then blessed be sentimentalism.

All idealism, let us repeat, rests on the spirituality of man, and that spirituality upon his immortality — and as for all these nothing of the nature of material proof is forthcoming, nothing beyond the circumstantial evidence of the soul, nothing of material proof is properly adducible against them.

That idealism has given bad reasons, does not disprove that it has the best of reasons for itself. It has made the mistake of giving materialistic authority for spiritual things; it is constantly stumbling over its own superstitions, and, in very truth, degenerating into sentimentalism.

As in religion, it pins its faith to old forms, and denies the formative energies of vital spiritual natures, so in art it will attach itself to certain periods and places and schools, and allow none other the seal of its approbation, forgetting that beauty has never yet been born so beautiful but that she must needs be born again.

Thus because beauty is known to have dwelt in Greece, it is fabled that there she laid down for ever in a marble tomb; or in Italy, maybe, we shall still find her haunting ancient cities; certain dead masters knew her secrets — but always we are taken to a grave. In some old palace, some old painting, some old book, it is that beauty lies buried; and if you boldly declare that you saw her rising, like Venus from the sea, in the soaring towers of New York, or heard her singing to herself, maybe, in Manchester — some one is sure to say, " Oh, no ! you must be mistaken; the age of beauty is past, the days of miracles are ended." On the face of every classic beauty has written the word " Resurgam," but those who watch in stupor by her tomb are not those who witness her resurrection. To such one day will come a startling touch upon the shoulder, and beauty already abroad in the world, with a strange morning light upon her face, will say, " I am not there — I am arisen."

How often does it prove that the so-called idealists are the materialists, the so-called materialists the only vital idealists. It is certainly true in religion, it is certainly true in art. Perhaps idealism is more often found where you would least expect it, among the so-called Philistines who build and bridge and victual the world; for we may be sure that Thebes was not the only city whose walls were built to music. The ugliest industrial city that ever blackened the blue sky and fouled the green earth was built to music too, else it had never been built at all. The most inveterate idealists I have ever met have been business men, and those are few who do not run their business in the interests of a dream — unacknowledged and perhaps even forgotten. There is a certain pathos in this, for such men have seldom a glimpse of their own poetry, — though they often have "literary" daughters, daughters who will babble idealism, while their fathers humbly practise it. We are never so near to the ideal as when we touch the real, and the gates of the spirit are in the walls of matter.

Either man is a spirit or he is the most ridiculous of all animals. Only an immortal destiny, an eternal significance, can justify his fantastic tricks before high heaven; and the

IDEALISM

supposed demolition of his spiritual pretensions by the criticism of science gave, as we have said, an opportunity to the cynic such as he had never before enjoyed in the history of mankind. The cup of man's humiliation was filled with the invention of the scientific novel, that so-called "realistic" presentation of human life which depicted only the physical side of the human paradox and degraded even that, reducing man and beast to a lowest common denominator of biology.

But it was of this final humiliation that the new idealism was to be born. Realism had now mistaken its function. So long as it had confined itself to correcting the mistakes of idealism, to discrediting its logic, to ridiculing its affectations, and generally criticising its formulæ, it was on safe ground; with ruthless industry it had done idealism the inestimable service of robbing it of all its bad old reasons for itself. Of its divinity and its pseudo-science, it was a competent critic; but there is one science idealism understands better than realism, — the science of human nature. It was when realism began to write novels, and from the criticism of human logic and human terminology proceeded to the analysis of the human heart, that idealism awoke with a laugh from the nightmare of despair into which German Biblical criticism and physical science had thrown it, and saw for the first time how shallow was the reasoning that would rob it of its dreams, saw that it had only been afraid of words all along.

This human nature!

Why, even the old waxworks of sentimentalism were truer to human nature than this *bête humaine*, this man, with all that made him man left out. Human nature — without worship, without dreams, without joy, without love! Realism! Could it be realism — which neglected to count these things among the realities?

Thus idealism set about examining some of the bogie words that had so alarmed it. Where it had talked of spirit, realism had opposed the word "matter" — and the heart of idealism, one hardly understands why, had incontinently sunk. Examining the word again, and the properties admitted to it, idealism began to understand that there was included amongst them a mysterious something, a mysterious central, vitalizing force, which even realism itself could not undertake to explain — and then a light broke in upon it. Why, this was but the spirit again, under another name. Instead of being something external to it, the spirit was perhaps an inherent property of every particle of matter.

In every pin-point of dust there might, indeed, be many other properties inimical to that little spark of soul, but that little spark that loved and dreamed was none the less undeniably there, and stood its eternal chance with the rest.

Thus it proved with all the words that had frightened it. They were but new words for its old intuitions, and in none of them, nor in any of the sciences or philosophies to which they belonged, was there really anything to terrify the soul of man.

They explained nothing — nor did they explain anything away. There was no science or philosophy, however "realistic," that did not leave the last word to be said by idealism. The universe had, indeed, been more accurately classified, but man had not really lost a single dream; on the contrary, his old dreams had been given back to him, augustly enlarged, dignified to a cosmic significance.

All the denials of materialistic science have but been preparing the way for a new and tremendous affirmation of the ideal, — an affirmation which must now have a value such as no affirmation of the ideal has ever possessed before. The value of a man's faith depends on the amount of doubt it holds in solution — and, similarly, the value of a man's idealism depends on the amount of ugliness it has been able to look upon and live. Idealism to be of any value to-day must be hard-wrung from the most thorough and uncompromising experience of existence. If you will call yourself an idealist — may I ask how many hard and ugly things have you faced? How deeply has sorrow wrung you? Have you known the unutterable bitterness of death? Have you looked into the bloody and vulgar face of war? Have you seen the cruel face of the sweater? Have you walked through hospitals? Have you listened without a fear to the last cold words of science?

Before you declare life good, and the soul of things beautiful, have you realised some-

IDEALISM

thing of these things? In the sweet cup you bring, have you thrown all the sours and bitters of the world, and has it yet remained sweet?

Only such an idealist is of any use to-day.

The old idealisms lost their authority because they did not know enough. Though actually based, as all idealisms must be, on little more than the *obiter dicta* of the human spirit that loves and worships and dreams, they were, as we have said, associated with antiquated theology and bad science.

Idealism, however, to-day, the idealism that is awakening the round world once more to a rejuvenescence of worship and wonder, romance and song, is well acquainted with the most pitiless biology and the most cynical documents of — French — human-nature. It knows all that realism can teach it — and far more. It is an idealism without illusions, it is an idealism that will wear.

It is, indeed, a very different thing from what our grandfathers meant by idealism — so different as perhaps hardly to be called by the same name. What our grandfathers meant is perhaps best suggested by that bad old verb " idealise." Our grandfathers actually found it necessary to "idealise" life, idealise this wonderful human life. They threw over it rose-lights from the outside. To them poetry and art were to be "improvements" upon, rather than pictures of and interpretations of, life, — as if the world was not more beautiful than anything that has ever been written about it. Like a fashionable photographer, they would smooth out all the wrinkles, touch up the eyes, complete with dimpled corners the cupid's bow of the mouth, and for the wonderful face of man, written over with joys and sorrows, with wistful eyes filled with eternal meanings, substitute a foolish image of simpering wax.

The new idealist, however, instead of throwing around life artificial light from the outside, is bent to reveal the inner shining that radiates for him from every object of human life and experience, however opaque it may at first seem; to tear away the veils of custom that obscure it; and to proclaim the essential wonderfulness and beauty — often enough a tragic beauty — of life, simply as life. Not

IDEALISM

life striking attitudes, or merely life heroic, romantic, or sentimental; but life anyhow and everywhere.

Not to "beautify" life, but to allow it to reveal its own beauty: that is the aim of the modern idealist, whether he be teacher or artist. The courageous and grateful acceptance, and the impassioned celebration of, the real, not the manufacture of insipid unrealities, — that is the mission of the new idealism. It includes moonlight as before, but it has realised in addition the picturesqueness of daylight.

The new idealism believes literally that miracles never cease; that the Golden Age is always with us; that the heroic age is never past; that human life in London and New York is just as poetical as it was in Rome or Florence; that God not only made the country, but that he also made the town; and if it cannot give us back our ancient heaven, it has, at all events, rediscovered for us the Earthly Paradise.

As an example of the sincerity, the thoroughness, of the new idealistic approach to life, one might instance the attitude of some of our young poets to the life of cities. London is the grim shepherdess, most in favour with the Tityrus of to-day, and, far from disdaining the steam-engine as prosaic, the modern poet asks nothing better for a subject. When Mr. Stephen Phillips writes of

> " The moonéd terminus through the dark
> With emerald and ruby spark,
> The stoker burningly embowered,
> With fiery roses on him showered," —

one hardly recognises Mr. Ruskin's abomination of desolation; and

> " Thou, merchant, or thou, clerk, hard driven, urged
> For ever on bright iron, timed by bells " —

would hardly know your tragic transfigured selves in Mr. Phillips' poetry.

Even the beauty of New York has been discovered by Mr. Charles G. D. Roberts, the very title of whose *New York Nocturnes* is a sign of how much idealism is already prepared to dare; while in far San Francisco a bright little *Lark* was recently heard singing the good news at Golden Gate to this melody: —

IDEALISM

"God, keep my youth and love alive, that I
  May wonder at this world until I die;
    Let sea and mountain speak to me, that so,
  Waking or sleeping, I may fight the lie; —
    Romance is dead, say some — but I say no!"

These lines I quote but as flowers blown before the breath of the spirit, feathers on the rising tide of the ideal, witnesses slight but significant of the growing tendency to find the ideal in the real, the poetry of life right in the very heart of its prose.

And this spring-wind of idealism is blowing its bird-voices about every land. Far away in Denmark painters are putting Paris behind them, and going back to those legends that are eternal symbols of the heart and lot of man. Germany, too, is once more awakening to a mystical art of strange fascination and significance. From Scotland and Ireland men come bringing fairy news in stories and songs. In Belgium Maeterlinck is seeing visions and clothing poignant realities in the garments of old dreams. Italy has her D'annunzio. Young France is romantic once more; and has not the most notorious of French realists recently proved himself what at heart he has always been, one of the noblest of idealists?

But this new idealism, we cannot be too careful to insist, is an idealism nourished on realities; on the real joys and real sorrows of real men and women. It is idealism not because it has shut its eyes to, but because it has faced, the real.

No doubt in course of time this new idealism will, like the old, ossify into formalism and sentimentalism, and a new era of realism be demanded to rectify its abuses, "and all the trial be gone o'er again."

Meanwhile, idealism has won one new friend of great importance, and needs to beware of one ancient enemy of great guile. The friend I mean is that tremendous ally — Woman: woman, who is always first to bite the apple of knowledge; woman the arch-idealist, mysterious harp vibrating ever earliest to the breath of the unseen. The poets and prophets of old time have had to save the world with but little help from their fellow-men. In future they will have woman to help them; woman able too to help them, as she has never been qualified to help them

IDEALISM

before; and women, too, by the thousand, thanks to what is significantly called their emancipation.

The emancipation of woman! What a history of what a slavery there is in the phrase. At one time a woman's views on life very properly went for little — as admittedly she was allowed to know so little about it; but to-day her comprehensive education, and the opportunities for reading modern authors afforded by her vast leisure, have changed all that, and the woman to-day who does n't know as much about life as a man is either a fool or a slave.

As for that subtle enemy of which I spoke: let me quote first this significant conclusion to a recent, most advanced book of philosophy: " Outside of spirit there is not, and there cannot be, any reality, and the more that anything is spiritual, so much the more is it veritably real."

Such words express the feeling, not only of the writer, but of all who are really thinking progressively to-day. Idealism is but another name for a great spiritual revival, one of those re-awakenings to consciousness of the human spirit that seem to come periodically in human history. Man once more grows unaccountably aware of the near presence of the divine, and conscious, with a certitude beyond argument, of a sanctity and majesty in his existence.

There is a wild young soul of faith hovering in the air, awaiting embodiment. And there is an ancient church with an enthralling history. It knows many secrets of the soul of man. It is fair to the eye, and sweet to the smell, and ravishing to the ear. It draws by the magic of many memories. Its doors are ever open, and all day long a voice calls out from among the pictures and the incense, — a voice very kind and full of rest. It promises an end of heartache, a putting off of burdens, and above all peace to the tortured brain. It demands in return but one offering, — the fearless mind of man.

O, idealists, beware how you enter there!

No old church is great enough for this mighty young spirit of faith, no merely imitative art. This spirit will make its own new churches, its own new art — only be patient, and fear not. Only give it time.

A DESULTORY NOTE ON VALUES

To any one who by grace of nature, or by taking thought, is able to regard human life with relatively ingenuous and unsophisticated eyes, nothing is more bewildering and indeed startling than the craziness of the scale of values regulating so-called important and unimportant things. Beginning maybe with a respectful faith that society must have arrived at its present curious method of assessment, in obedience to a long series of observations the law of which we have yet to master, and, indeed here and there coming upon false values in which we dimly discover the fading traces of values once real but no longer life-giving and long since forgotten, we, nevertheless, soon realise that it is not law we have to consider but an anarchy in which the active element is vulgarity and the passive superstition. Broadly speaking, vulgarity has made our prices and superstition keeps them up.

One of the dreams of the German philosopher Nietzsche was to make what he called a Transvaluation of all the Values. Perhaps he was hardly the man to do it, perhaps no one man would be the man to do it, for value, though perhaps mainly a recognition of innate precious qualities in certain objects and moments and activities, is also to a certain degree a social hall-mark — though only to be allowed as such when the society is mainly composed of units capable of apprehending real and not merely false values.

What is a real and what is a false value? Without delaying to make all those qualifications which every definition demands, we might hazard that that is a real value which is real to our sincere selves and at the same time accepted as real by the finest spirits of the race.

Happily society is not without examples of approximately real valuation. It is a principle of just valuation which makes us pay great musicians and singers at the rate of a fortune a week. Such principle also regulates

A NOTE ON VALUES

the salaries of beautiful actresses, many of whom are very properly paid for nothing but being beautiful and allowing us to look upon them. The compellers of laughter and the drawers of tears of just right are housed in palaces and luxurious castellated flats. In a world so poor in laughter, priceless indeed is the stored mirth in the heart of a Penley.

It was an approach to just valuation when the other day the manuscript of Keats' *Endymion* was sold for several hundred pounds though it will be observed that the sum was about four times as much as Keats received for his poetry during his lifetime, and that the money went into the pockets of the descendants, not of the poet, but of his publisher. Poetry, one need hardly say, provides the most significant example of false valuation. Poets and prophets are the most important people to a community — after the comedians whom they occasionally rival — and yet curiously enough they are the worst paid. The fact of being poets and prophets is sufficient pay in itself, you may say — no doubt, but the same would apply to the beauties and the comedians.

In thus emphasising the value of laughter I have had in my mind a phrase of Stevenson which any of us ambitious to start out upon a Re-valuation of all the values might take with him as an excellent touchstone. It occurs, if I remember aright, in *The Amateur Emigrant*, in which, describing one of his fellow passengers in his voluntary "second cabin" voyage to America, he tells us of his ambitions for commercial and civic success. He spoke of such success, adds Stevenson, with one of those flashes of reality which make him something like a great writer — "as if it was real like laughter."

"As if it was real like laughter"!

What a profound saying is that! — how clear-seeing, how purged must have been the vision of the man who could look right through the thousand obscuring veils of custom and sham, to light up with so vivid a phrase the reality behind.

Well, in that phrase Stevenson laid the foundation stone of a new philosophy which each of his books went to illustrate. And it might be described as the philosophy of knowing what one really cares about in life, not what we are told to care about, what we are too apt really to fancy we do care about, — a philosophy of real values based on the actual and not the imaginary desires of human beings. There are a number of dull things we do, a number of dull successes we strive for, with seldom a thought of how dull they are to the real self which dreams and plays in our neglected souls. And I am venturing to speak not merely for a handful of dreamers and idealists, the professors of the emotions and the senses, but for the bulk of men and women.

Take the most resoundingly successful of these, and, if you can induce them to be momentarily honest, you will find that to themselves in their heart of hearts the *raison d'être* of their lives is not the exterior achievement of it, not the conquests of their intellect, nor the triumphs of their skill, not the decorations of their success, but just some simple moments of emotion, some few snatched hours of play.

Indeed, man is at heart a dreamer who has forgotten his dream. Centuries ago he dreamed it, as he dreams it over again in the heart of every young man and woman, dreamed it fervently and longed to build it.

But the building materials were so costly, so hard to win, the labour of building so great, that soon he became entirely absorbed in these and went on toilfully building, quite forgetting why he built. Then when the dream was built, he moved into it with his wife and children, and dwelt therein in a commonplace way, valuing only the cost of the structure and the furniture of the dream, and forgetting the dream itself. But sometimes a poet will come to dinner, and as the bourgeois man looks into his simple eyes, suddenly the scales fall from his own and he starts up for a wonderful moment of reality, and a sweet old voice cries in his ears, as he looks on his wife and his home: "This habit, why, it was once a passion — this fact, why, it was once a dream!"

In its heart the world cares for little but play; but in its life it does hardly anything but work, for the world has forgotten that the reason of its work is — play. The natural man works that he may play — works that he may love and dream, and know while he may the wonders and joys of the strange and lovely world which for a short space he is allowed to inhabit; the unnatural man plays that he may work.

So unnatural indeed have we become that not only have we forgotten our dreams, but we have actually grown ashamed of them. Proverbially there is nothing of which an Englishman is so much ashamed as his emotions. To suspect him of sentiment is to imply insult, to surprise him in tears is to commit a mortal offence. Laughter he still retains, but too often for the unworthy purpose of laughing at other people's emotions, and ridiculing beautiful things he no longer understands. England indeed is the Siberia of the emotions.

As an example of our attitude toward the emotions, consider the universal treatment of that widespread class, the lovers of a community. As they go by through the streets hand in hand, a dream-fed, flower-crowned company -

> "Speaking evermore among themselves
> Their heart-remembered names" —

do we bow the knee and doff our hats as they pass; do we strew their path with roses; do we clear the way for their beautiful faces; do we say to ourselves: "Hush! there go the holy ones, the lovers, the great dreamers, the young priests and priestesses of futurity."

No. We hunt them with little boys, we startle them in shy corners with lights, we break upon their delicate reveries with ruthless laughter. Poor harried dreamers — their dream will be short-lived enough at the best.

So it is we despitefully use the very important people who are some day to fill our armies, man our ships, populate our offices; and who, if they fulfilled no such practical services to the state, would be valuable public servants in that they keep the world young, and by their transcendental antics remind us that man does not live by company-promoting alone.

SO THIS IS AMERICA

So this is America!

No, you say, this is only New York, and as yet your highly Europeanised hotel protects you from America. This is the city to which all the ends of the earth are come. This is Cosmopolis, not America!

I suppose every country possesses these pedantic aborigines who will recognise nobody for a Roman who is not a direct descendant of Æneas, and who limit the representatives of a country to some oligarchic four hundred, or some shaggy and violent primitives of its western mines, — men who recognise nothing later than origins and deny developments.

Of course we have them in England — men who will tell you that Liverpool and Manchester, nay, even London, are not England, and that the true English type is only to be studied in the dreaming quadrangles of Oxford, or the sleeping cloisters of cathedral cities. Similarly I have met charming old gentlemen who recognise no English literature later than *Beowulf*, and reserve the term " good English " for Saxon words of one syllable.

It is a curious logic. That a country began in one place would seem to be the best of all reasons for its ending in another. America began in Boston. Since then it has developed into a thousand equally characteristic cities. Some day — being a swift goer — it may even catch up to Chicago.

Meanwhile, the present writer has arrived at New York, and as he has already met with quite a number of Americans here and encountered various fashions and modes of being that strike him as being neither European, Asiatic, nor African, he must be forgiven for concluding that they are American; and shall venture to ask: if one cannot say " America is here or nowhere " in New York where must one dare to say it? Whither then, O Goddess of Liberty, must I follow your flying feet?

No doubt the American eagle has many nests, but surely in New York, too, one may hear its protecting scream, and on Broadway and Fifth Avenue pick up characteristic examples of its feathers.

I think an American would smile if he could hear the various precautions imposed upon an Englishman who would visit America. They are hardly less nervous and elaborate than in the days when our grandfathers used to make their wills before facing the perils of a fifty-mile coach journey.

The American customs — the American interviewer — the American winter — the American inconvenience and incivility — the American child — American noise; these are some of the terrors which appal the stout heart that would make these Lavinian shores.

Well, I have faced them all — and I still survive to tell the tale. If my experiences are unsensational compared with that of my countrymen, one must not forget that there is a class of travellers who would seem to visit foreign countries for the purpose of complaining that they are not at home, who expect to do at Rome what *Home* does; then again all nationalities number travelling representatives who are neither philosophers nor gentle-

men, people who always make the maximum of
fuss on the minimum of occasion, fastidious
souls who can never find any thing "fit to
eat" in any hotel of any kind, men and
women who seem to think the world was
created as a feather bed for their miserable
bodies.

I met one of these poor ill-used gentry an
evening or two ago in the smoking-room of a
hotel, in which to my thinking he was the only
objectionable thing. In a world so warmly
provided with comfortable and friendly hotels,
it would be indiscreet and indeed ungrateful
to declare it the most comfortable or the most
friendly; but it is certainly to be placed among
the first dozen of ideal hotels. Every comfort
and convenience of which one can conceive
are there — even civility. But my companion
complained bitterly of a different experience.
For him it was a "beastly hole" — "nothing
fit to eat" — "no attention;" and he was
off to-morrow — of all countries — to Spain,
which he declared "the only country in which
a gentleman could live." For the first time as
he spoke I feared the probability of war with
Spain.

He himself, I was glad to remember, was not an Englishman, belonging as he did to an ancient race of professional wanderers, who so far have been able to make themselves comfortable in any country: a race noble and honourable, but occasionally unfortunate, like any other, in its representatives; and by the number of times he spoke the word "gentleman" in ten minutes, and his manner of ordering some cigarettes from the waiter, I understood what was the matter with the hotel and with him.

This is a digression, and yet, I think, not without bearing upon that vexed question, — the writing of American impressions. If the present writer's impressions are for the moment optimistic, he does not forget nor wish it forgotten that they are scarcely a fortnight old. They are, therefore, occupied with the simplest and most elementary matters, those superficial considerations which necessarily first strike a stranger as he lands at a foreign port and treads a foreign shore. I write but of my American matriculation.

When I have passed the American Custom-House a littler oftener I may revise my opinion of the geniality of its officers. Meanwhile I can only record one individual experience of good fortune. Of course things might well have been different, had my wife and I belonged to that criminal class which wear international sealskin. As it was, however, our officer proved an angel and an American humourist combined. He did not strew the cobbles and sawdust of the wharf with my wife's gowns, nor did he make any objection to reasonable changes of raiment. He even added compliment to courtesy.

My wife had but one new hat — she said. She was sure there could be no need to examine that? Oh, but our Mark Twain of an exciseman was just dying to see it. "And I'm sure," he said, "you're just longing for a sight of it yourself, after all this time, and your terrible passage across."

How could one deny him?

"Well, it's a bute," he said, "a perfect bute! Now I'm sure you're grateful to me for another look at it." And I'm sure she was.

So did we pass the dreaded American customs.

SO THIS IS AMERICA

From them we passed into the dreaded American winter. This wonderful sunshine — winter! Free champagne, we ventured to call it. It was true that snow lay all about and it was evidently snow of an arctic stubbornness, though it was but two or three inches deep. I gathered that it had resisted the efforts of the New York scavengers for some three days, and to judge by the way in which it lay about in rutted drifts across the roadway you might have thought it had remained there as it fell. No doubt snow in London melts more quickly — at all events it disappears as it does not seem to disappear in New York.

Perhaps it was only picture-snow! The sunshine and the mildness of the air seemed to suggest that explanation. At all events we felt our fur coats a little cowardly, and that was our first impression of American winter.

But I find I have forgotten the American interviewer. How ungrateful of me!

I know that really great people always refuse to be interviewed. However, I was content to be an exception. A good old rule of manners is to do in America as the Americans do. Therefore it seemed to me merely courteous to be interviewed. Could I, with politeness, not to speak of humanity, allow these intelligent and charming gentlemen to stand about that draughty and cobbled quay in vain? They were kind enough to be interested in me. Why should I pretend that I did not share their interest? It would have been the paltriest of affectations. I am interested in myself, as every author born of a publisher is, and I am not only not indifferent, but positively grateful that man born of woman should be interested in me, too. I don't write books for the purpose of hushing them up. I want them heard of, I want them read, I am not above allowing them to be bought.

If these gentlemen who lie in wait for unpunctual Atlantic liners on draughty quays on wintry mornings will help me to that — why should I, being little, ape greatness by denial of them, or being great, imitate littleness by turning up my nose at one of the most efficient methods of that publication which any one with any thing to say should not be too proud to welcome?

SO THIS IS AMERICA

The gods speak to mortals through many channels; of old through the oracles of Eleusis, to-day through the American interviewer. That the divine messages are liable to fantastic distortion in the process of communication is but one of the conditions attaching to all human instruments. The American interviewer does his best, and when you consider the number and variety of phenomena, human and otherwise, on which he must pose as an authority, it is impossible not to have sympathy for him, however cruelly he may have misunderstood you.

I now come to American inconvenience and incivility. Well, so far as my week or two's experience goes I would unhesitatingly drop off the prefix in both cases. When my English friends spoke of inconvenience they were, I fancy, mainly thinking of hansoms.

Certainly one misses those — that is, one misses the London eight-penny fare. Yet if it is true that hansoms here are, say twice as expensive, it is also true that on those occasions when in New York you chiefly need them, occasions of pleasure, *tête-à-tête* occasions, you don't much mind the extra cost;

and for the more necessitous purposes of getting home, getting about the city, the cable car more than makes up for the high-priced hansom. The cable car terrifies one at the crossings, but when I want to get back to my hotel in half the time I could do it in London I thank heaven for the monopoly which keeps the busiest thoroughfare in New York, a city busier to the square inch of its cramped situation than London, so remarkably uncongested and so conveniently free from merely personal and speculative traffic. That there ought to be more cars and less straps I don't deny, and yet the manner in which the cars are crowded seems to me to bring out a winning element of the American character, — its freedom from fussiness, from red-tape, when something has to be done.

When America — I mean New York — wants to keep an appointment, or when New York wants to get home, it does n't mind hanging on to a strap for twenty minutes, so long as it gets there in time; and, realising that its neighbour is similarly bent, it does n't frown at him for pushing or crowding a little in his haste. I seem to see here a certain boyishness in the American character, a certain touch of what in England we call "the casual," which appeals to me; and the manner in which a conductor methodically collects fares from passengers hanging on behind the car, who in England would be scared off with an oath or a by-law, is to me one of the constant delights of travel by the cable car. Still, a seat once out of every ten journeys would, I grant, appeal to me, too.

Civility here, I fancy, as in other countries, is the child of courtesy, and as for convenience — well, at all events, there is no lack of conveniences.

The American child! I made her first acquaintance in this manner: Desiring to use the hotel telephone, I approached the box with the trepidation of a man whose country, shall we say, always waits for the very latest improvements before it adopts a time- or space-saving invention. That is, being an Englishman, I am not accustomed to the telephone. Well, the operator said I must wait, as there was one ahead of me for whom he was engaged in making a connection. Meekly I waited, and while doing so became aware of a very little girl standing near me, hair down to her waist, frock up to her knees — but, oh, with such cold young eyes!

Could it be possible that this uncannily self-possessed little creature was the person to whom the operator referred?

Indeed it was, for presently the man offered her the tube, and taking it from him with the most imperturbable *sang froid*, she closed the door of the box, sat down, and began to talk to her unseen friend. Evidently she was arranging her next dinner party! No doubt the American will say, "Why not?" and certainly it is better that children should begin early to take their own part and find their own way about in the world, instead of blushing their way through a gauche and timorous childhood. Nevertheless, I confess that that little girl rather frightened me. Nothing so much as that cold young look of hers has made me feel that I belong to an effete and kindly civilisation.

American noise! No doubt New York knows how to be noisy, but I gather that the first youth of its noise has now passed. A more humane method of pavement is gradually driving the dryads and fauns of noise into the side streets and the polyglot quarters. On Fifth Avenue, at all events, you can hardly detect a sound. However, it is not to be hoped, though it is hardly to be feared, that New York will become too quiet; for the noise of a great city is its characteristic voice, which to those who know and love it becomes endeared. At first the noise of a great city is merely noise — bewildering, buffeting, and somewhat menacing. We are as yet ignorant of the meaning of all these unfamiliar sounds, whence and why they come. But presently, as we grow more accustomed to it, this noise is changing into music, — we begin to detect a harmony, and before long can follow the beat of its rhythms.

Was it not so when first we came to London, and stood deafened and clutching on to a policeman in some maelstrom of the traffic? Yet how soon had the noise died down into music, — the siren song of the city that we love.

So I conceive it must be with New York. Already I seem to be learning some of the notes, and sometimes as I wake in the small hours I go to my window just to catch the never-ending song of the cables humming on through the listening night, like the sound of brooks running underground.

Already, too, I love, while I fear, that other noise, that Chinese "snickersnee" clang of the cable cars. As yet I have not become educated up to the Wagnerian melodies of the Elevated Railroad, — but I must remind you once more of how short a time I have been here. I am convinced that some poet who loves New York, as one or two of our young poets love London, would have no difficulty in compelling even the Elevated to some "utterance of harmony."

But what about New York buildings? What of Brooklyn Bridge? Yes, I have beheld these wonders, — those soaring altitudes of stone, that morning gossamer of iron. Such engineering epics — or rather lyrics — as Brooklyn Bridge I did America the compliment of expecting. My mind is simple enough to take merely material marvels for granted — in America, *par excellence* the Country of Applied Ideas. The real beauty and excellent taste in the buildings surprised me more. I have seen buildings that only need to have been born in Italy to make their fortunes, and everywhere I have been struck with the dignified simplicity in the use of stone and iron and wood. It is seldom that one is offended by cheap and nasty ornament. If American architects have not risked the exuberances of originality, they have known how to keep quiet. They can leave beautiful smooth stone alone, at least leave it still smooth and beautiful. They have learned the lesson of William Morris as it is only just being learned in England, with the result that Fifth Avenue, with the collaboration of the exquisitely vivid atmosphere, is surely a vista of great beauty and nobility, worthy of the wide-browed, calm-eyed, beautiful women who sweep along it, very evidently the imperious daughters of an imperial nation.

Yes, in the modern way, I would certainly call New York beautiful; particularly at night, when you stand near Central Park, say about Fifty-seventh Street, and from the rise of the hill watch the theatres and shops and sky-signs of Broadway glittering like a crown of many-coloured jewels. But, indeed, what city could fail to seem beautiful in such an atmosphere?

Still more than any external characteristic, as I walk New York streets the impression that mainly arrests me is one entirely unillustratable by particulars, an impression of moral seriousness and youthful energy combined. As old cities seem to exhale senility, so this young city seems to exhale a vernal breath. Young blood seems to palpitate through the streets. Indefinably, at every corner, through all its avenues, there comes sweeping about one a certain sense that this is a young nation sternly in earnest. It is a nation that means business, it will stand no nonsense; it is a nation in which, to borrow a phrase from a certain quack-prophet of Germanity — "the drones must die."

With this, too, I gain an equally indefinable impression, such as I have never received in countries equally liable to conscription, that this is a nation of soldiers. Many of these busy men about me have been soldiers already, and all are eager at a moment's notice to become soldiers — soldiers of the American Idea. The American eagle is indeed very strong and very young. If I were a popular preacher or a popular actor, I would courageously cross my metaphor and declare it the worthy offspring of the British lion.

But, after all, America, like any other country, is good or bad as thinking makes it so. I confess that I came to it with prejudices of old gratitude, gratitude to a land which had produced some of the books that have best helped me in the difficult business of living. To me it was dear before I saw it, for the sake of Emerson and Thoreau and Walt Whitman, and for the sake, too, of essayists like Washington Irving and William Winter, whose books I have carried so often through Warwickshire lanes. We may respect a country for its battles, we may conquer it for its women, but we can only love it for its books.

POETRY AND THE JUBILEE

THERE seems to be no trade or profession in her Majesty's dominions which is not taking new courage, cherishing fantastic hopes, because it chances to be just alive in this year of especial grace, 1897. A great loosening of the heart and the purse-strings is evidently anticipated — indeed, by the catering classes, one might say, expected. All who minister to human comfort or convenience genially expect to be paid fifty times their usual charges for their ministrations — "so hallowed and so gracious is the time." To be alive in this halcyon year is luck, to be born in it a sort of greatness, to die in it sanctification. An officiating clergyman — which is polite for officious — gravely congratulated a bride and bridegroom the other day on being married in this honourable year. They were twice blest; and purchasers of a certain port, one reads with envy, are to be

POETRY AND THE JUBILEE

made happy with special labels stating that the wine was bought in the Diamond Jubilee year. May not poor poetry, therefore, presume to be "like things of the season gay," and pretend to itself that its long-deferred millennium is at hand? For as many thousand years as the world has lasted, poetry has picked up a precarious existence, a suspected mendicant art, suffering and suffered, living desperately between kicks and halfpence, a tattered Apollo feeding the pigs — or the public: is it too much to hope that in this blessed year of jubilee it may share in some of the luck of its more important fellows, catch at least a few of the crumbs falling from the table of the wise? I say wise, because to be wealthy is surely to be wise. To be poor is man's only folly.

Is it too much to hope? Too much to hope — that the world which sent blind Homer a beggar-man through its cities, and has starved or silenced every poet since, except those who had inheritances or relations — fortunately larger in number than is usually supposed — is going at this time of day to begin keeping its poets? Too much to hope!

POETRY AND THE JUBILEE

Why, of course, it is merely absurd, quite stark staring mad even to mention it. But then everyone else seems to have gone stark staring mad in this blessed year of the blessed Jubilee — so why not our poets?

Yes, it is a dream, and it will come true — when one of Mr. Bernard Shaw's plays runs for a hundred nights. Still, dreams are the poet's all; so let us, for a little, speculate on the poet's wildest hope — to be fed. To be fed, not for idleness, but, like every other worker, for the service he does the community. That is a curious popular error, that of the idleness of poets. As a matter of fact there is no business man, however great his concerns, who is a tithe so hard-worked as a responsible poet. The quality of his work entails no such wear and tear of the whole being, no such pitiless waste of all the tissues, no such deadly tension of the nerves, as the work of the poet; work, too, which never ceases, from the tragic moment when the poet first sees the light, to the thankful "it is finished" when he closes for ever his weary smitten eyes. He who works for eternity must waste himself in a word.

POETRY AND THE JUBILEE

But perhaps the reader is inclined to question the value of this "work," to ask, as the landlady asked Mr. Wilson Barrett's "Chatterton," "What's the use of poetry?" Of course it is open to any individual to rate that value and use as he pleases; but of the national opinion on the subject there can be no question. The nation may decline to support its poets, but it is none the less proud of them — perhaps all the more, because they cost so little. Is England prouder of anything than its literature? Yet how much has it contributed to its support? The English Navy, the English Army, and English Literature — these are the three feathers in the national cap; but think what England pays for her army and her navy, and look up in "Whitaker's" how much she spends on her literature. Of course literature is not in its nature so expensive a distinction, but, relatively to the necessities of support, will any one contend that it is nationally supported at all?

Why not disendow the Church, and endow Literature, which is really the Coming Church? No doubt our literary men all round would be content to accept a thousand a year from the State, and allow the State to recoup itself out of their profits.

However, that is a proposal more appropriate for the Millennium than the Jubilee. It is wild even for the Diamond Jubilee. Therefore I will address my remarks less to the nation than to the nation's millionaires. On them devolves the glory of fastening in the memory of time, by a variety of monumental beneficence, the honourable characteristics of the longest and most progressive reign in English history. In many directions the Victorian era has surpassed and amassed like no era before it. This is perhaps sufficiently acknowledged. It is acknowledged too, that in nothing has it juster reason to pride itself than in its literature. Well, then, is there to be no adequate " Jubilee " recognition of the fact? Is that which will remain an honour bright and contemporary when so many honours vaunted to-day lie silent beneath the dust of the antique — is that noble and generous art which not only immortalises itself, but immortalises all that has once moved within the circle of its light, gener-

POETRY AND THE JUBILEE

ous even in its lasting youth to the dead and gone prides, the faded pomps, the decrepit powers that used to put it by; to that alone which honours all the rest — are there to be no honours this most honourable year?

Let us whisper this to the millionaire — the thing you dread most is to be forgotten, your secret hope is to found a house, to leave a name. There are other ways. You may go on living after death associated hospitably with some terrible disease which men shudder to say — cancer, epilepsy, paralysis of the spine; you may give to your native city a park, where greasy loafers will spit all day upon your name; you may eternalise your frock-coat in disagreeable stone; or you may sink unthanked-for fortunes in raising those towers of desolation called workmen's dwellings, in which the workmen refuse to dwell: these and other ways there are to be memorably forgotten; but would you wear a laurel that never fades, would you have your name smell sweet with the myrrh of remembrance, and chime melodiously in the ear of future days, make haste, O millionaire, make haste, and pray some poet put your name into his song!

He will do it for so little, for he is a grateful heart. For what you carelessly pay for a window to view the procession you could buy his reverberating gratitude through all eternity. Buy! Why not? Gratitude must always be bought with something — and what should buy it so fairly as money? I saw some poor literary man advertising the other day for £100 to give him a year's rest from Grub-street, that he might devote himself to a piece of real work. I have wondered since if he got it. Does any one suppose for a moment that he did? And yet I heard, too, the other day that there are £900,000,000 in English banks bored with having nothing to do. Our whole civilisation reeks — and rots — with wealth. We can pay a club £6,000 for its windows, and yet there is no one to risk £100 on a possible genius, who, poor soul, must be no spendthrift if he knows how to buy "a year's rest" — O healing phrase, as of wells and palm trees! — for a poor £100.

Millionaires, O millionaires! I will not say that the poets of your land are starving in

POETRY AND THE JUBILEE

garrets. No; but they are driven to playwriting — which is perhaps worse for their genius — to playwriting, and book-reviewing, and the fifty other forms of keeping the herds of Admetus. One of them is simply dying, artistically, because he has never seen Italy; another has a new Divine Comedy dark and bitter within him — but who can be a Dante in his spare hours? A third would bring back the muses to Ireland, a fourth has found the lost keys of hope and faith, and there are others with other messages and dreams, very important, even to millionaires. No doubt these men will do their work without your help, will speak in spite of all the iron forces of silence, but, oh! your help were sweet! A year's rest for these men, O millionaires, a year's rest — to work in. How easy it were for you to give them all five years' rest — to work in, mind! — a whole life's rest. With the stroke of a pen you could endow all the genius that deserves and needs endowment; you could be the virtual founders of Twentieth Century English Literature! £50,000 invested at 4 per cent would provide eight poets with £250 a year for life, and it would be easy to double it, and thus allow them a wife and two children apiece. What is £50,000, — what even is £100,000, — seriously speaking, to pay for the honour of doing so great a service to your country? You hesitate? Yet were you asked for such a contribution towards national sport, you would write the cheque without a word. It is well that you should do something for the national muscles, but will you do nothing for the national brains?

For the other arts something is done, sometimes a good deal. For scholars and philosophers there are scholarships and fellowships, for composers and painters there are also scholarships and travelling stipendia. For literary men, except when they have failed, there is practically nothing. The popular literary arts need no assistance; novelists live in castles, build mansions for themselves, and are generally self-supporting. The one exception to the fate of poets out of all the ages, Tennyson, did the same; but for the most part poets must either be supported, or, in the process of earning their honest livings, surely and swiftly cease to be poets. The American

POETRY AND THE JUBILEE

philosopher John Fiske has wisely said that " the last thing one should ask a philosopher to do is to support himself." The remark applies with greater force to the poet, whose temperament unfits him even more than the philosopher from practising his art and getting his living at the same time: for you must remember it is not the time for the mere writing that the poet needs — you can always find time to write — it is the time to live in which the poet is so poor, the time to see and feel, to love and hate, to learn men and women, to read wise old books, to see old pictures and new lands, to take solitary walks, to riot in company — time to laugh, to weep; in brief, not merely the time to write, but the time to live something worth writing about.

Millionaires, it is this time you can buy for your country's poets — buy so easily, if you will, that it makes the heart ache to think of it. This is the blessed year of the Diamond Jubilee; will you not make it originally remarkable beyond any year out of all time by taking the suggestion I offer? It has, I know, been made before in vain, but then it was not the year of the Diamond Jubilee.

The better the year the better the deed. Done this year, the act will shine with a double lustre. It is better than an ugly house in Park-lane, believe me; and then, of course, you can still have that too. Have you not said that you would spend more on your stables than the sum I ask? Or if one of you cannot see your way, how about a syndicate of Mæcenases? And, at all events, make a beginning by endowing a fund to send a young poet once a year to Italy. Thus alone will you win an easy immortality, and show an originality in the spending of your money which will lift you at once out of the mere rabble of millionaires. Millionaires, O millionaires! can you not be pioneers as well as millionaires?

THE LESSON OF ROMEIKE

I BEGAN to subscribe to a press-cutting agency from an innocent hope of instruction. I have continued my subscription for amusement. It was no doubt boyish to hope that a young writer, who could hardly expect to start his career as an immediate and impeccable master, but would need, often by humiliating failure, to learn much of his art by the way, might perhaps learn something of that art from such confident and consummate professors of it as his critics were likely to be.

It is true that the critics of the past did not greatly encourage one in this hope; but then the critics of the present always learn by the mistakes of the critics of the past, and this was a liberal, experimental age, to which new art was gallantly declared welcome.

Well, of course, it was love's young dream of literature, and the lesson I was to learn from Romeike was something quite different. Now, when I know so well what to expect, it seems so strange that I should ever have thought that critics should love or even know literature; that they should be eager to give one a helping hand rather than feverishly, if vainly, anxious to stamp one out of existence; or that they should even observe such a simple law of the game as fair play. I am here, of course, speaking of critics generally; to this rule of disillusion there are exceptions, as to every other; critics whose praise one can accept, critics for whose censure one can be grateful.

But, for the most part, the subscriber to Romeike must expect to pay, not for criticism, but for the most strange and bewildering jumble puzzle of tastes and opinions, and certainly a most fantastic presentment of his own poor self and doings. If you care to hear in the same breath that your writings are the purest and the filthiest ever penned, that they are at once rollicking with merriment and entirely devoid of humour, that they are reverent to a fault, and profane beyond belief — by all means subscribe to Romeike.

If, again, it entertains you to read that you do your writing in a balloon and only come

THE LESSON OF ROMEIKE

down for meals, wear one side of your hair blue and the other yellow, that you likewise wear corsets, and that your real name is Jones, then again I say by all means subscribe to Romeike.

These diversities of opinion and distortions of personality do, I confess, entertain me. This figmentary self at once delights and affrights me — this monstrous self no other glass has ever shown me, no friend of mine has ever seen.

Besides, this imaginary self has its uses. It is one's whipping-boy. While the slings and arrows are at work on the unfortunate phantom of oneself, the real self walks in a sunny cloister, unconscious of the clamour; and if sometimes an echo of the tumult reaches there, or if, indeed, blows fall on the cloister door and one's name flies through on opprobrious breath, the real self smiles and shakes its head, it never dreams that *it* is meant. "Not here, dear friends," it murmurs; "it must be the other fellow of the same name."

We are all more or less agreed that personal temperament and predilection must play an unavoidable part in all criticism; but it is not till you subscribe to Romeike that you realise how great is that part; that, in fact, the part thus played is practically the whole. At all events, it is no exaggeration to say that literary opinion is formed nine-tenths on considerations which have nothing whatever to do with literature, but have to do with a man's milieu, his training, his religion, his family connections, his health, his habits, particularly his temper, and fifty other considerations, even before we approach relevancy in personal literary antipathies, attractions, tastes, and judgments.

I am not complaining of this. Literature was made for man, and not man for literature, and man has a right to ask that the chaos of man shall be fully represented in the cosmos of literature. He has a right to ask that his own particular narrowness, among all the other narrownesses that go to make up the abstraction humanity, shall find hearing and expression somewhere in literature; and it is but natural that he should judge literature according to the faithfulness with which it expresses and regards that narrowness.

That one might be suspected of complaining arises from the involuntary assumption that a good book must of necessity seem a good book to everybody. This, of course, is far from being the case. A classic is not a classic for all classes. Even the Bible is not a good book east of Suez. Indeed, for young readers it is not fit reading in any country. Dickens, perhaps, is no longer a classic west of Trafalgar-square. England still regrets Fielding, and keeps Shakespeare in his place by sheer dint of not reading him. Men still desire to kick Sterne. Lamb is a weariness to many young people, and Tennyson is as a tale that is told. Heine is still the devil in many literary cosmogonies. Shelley, despite his monument, is "bad form" at Oxford to this day, and Keats is still the nasty, mawkish surgeon's apprentice. Thus, and in a thousand other ways, must tastes for ever differ; and not only must the old tastes differ, but new tastes and distastes must arise with each new generation further to complicate the critical situation.

The two kinds of change which most fundamentally affect literature are, of course, changes in ethical and political ideals; and it is with regard to the ethical and political conditions of the moment, that that tremendous question of the "good taste" of a given book will be decided simultaneously for and against it — for the moment. Perhaps a good general rule of consolation in this matter is that the conventional good taste of the present is the bad taste of the future. It was once in shocking taste to say that the earth moved round the sun. It was once the best of form for gentlemen to talk like stable-boys and to be carried to bed drunk each evening. It was once in shocking taste to say that the Book of Genesis is a fairy tale. It was once the best of form for gentlemen to murder each other on the slightest provocation. It is still in shocking taste to criticise the spoliation of the poor by the rich. It is still the best of form for a husband to shoot his wife because she has transferred her affections to another more interesting and more amiable man. In fact, it has always been bad taste to question the current fallacies of the day, however childish and dangerous, and always good form to observe the current attitudes and manners of the day, however disgusting, imbecile, and cruel.

Now, any time since the French Revolution there has been a steady warfare waging between two ethical ideas and two political ideas, between Christian asceticism and modern humanism — the gospel of the joy of life — on the one hand, and between the aristocratic and democratic ideas on the other.

These ethical and political ideas have mutually interacted beneath the surface, so that what is valuable in Christianity has passed into democracy, and all that was good in aristocracy — those secrets of humanism which it had wealth and leisure to learn — have passed into the humanist gospel; but on the surface Christianity and aristocracy are still ranged together against democracy and humanism, the dead bodies against the life that once animated them.

Once upon a time Christianity stood for most of the purity and pity that existed in the world, and aristocracy, perhaps, stood for most of the world's refinement and culture; but that time has passed, and at the present moment both goodness and good breeding, to state it gently, are quite as likely to be found elsewhere.

The application of these remarks to the student of Romeike will speedily become apparent if he should happen to have written an imaginative book (romance or poem, whatever it may be) on that cardinal subject of imaginative literature — Love. It chances that just now the ethical situation on this great, serious, beautiful, and humorous subject is divided as it has never been before. With the decay of Christian asceticism Love has dared to speak as it has only dared to think before; it has, in the most refined and intelligent quarters, come to discard the impurity of silence for the purity of speech, and to realise what it has long ventured to suspect: that it is not certain facts and manifestations of its simple nature, but its enforced reticence upon them that is unclean.

It is to these ideas that any one concerned with a living " good taste " will defer; but he will not be alarmed or unhappy if the numerically larger party, who by no means think so, but who, indeed, aghast at the emancipation of such ideas, have rushed for safety to reactionary extremes of reticence and hypocrisy — if such assail him with irrelevant nouns of

THE LESSON OF ROMEIKE 139

abuse, which but rebound upon those — relevant nouns — who use them.

If he is true to himself he will wish for nothing better than such decisive dissociation of his name by the lips of those who still hold to ideals of antique brutality and uncleanness.

It is obvious that if such a book be written by one who professes that progressive "good taste," and should fall into the hands of a reviewer who holds to a reactionary "good taste," the chances of the book being considered as literature are small. Nor, perhaps, is it necessarily the reviewer's duty to consider the book as literature. Its importance as a danger to those ideals of morality sacred to the reviewer, may seem such that he feels it his duty to attack it uncompromisingly in that character. One will not object to that, if the man's honest. But if, on the other hand, the man's a liar, if he wilfully misrepresents the book by an exhibition of dead quotations, — quotations whose life and character have gone with the atmosphere in which they were created to breathe, and which now merely stink in the putrefying air of the reviewer's own mind, — what then? Well, nothing then. The thing is a low personal assault, a criminal defamation of literary character, and the proper place to take it would be the Old Bailey; but unfortunately there is no Old Bailey for the Criminal Reviewer, though, to judge by the amount of mere personal ruffianism and dirty blood which is allowed to pass for criticism, one cannot but think that the ranks of critical journalism are largely recruited from the criminal classes.

Still, baseness is surely not going to dismay you. The passage of new ideas to acceptance is always attended by much unsavory dislodgement of the circumambient air; in the wake of any speed there is always a flutter of dirty paper. Besides, there is a genuine pleasure in thinking of the agreeable excitement or notoriety which you have been the means of winning for some sad little scribbler, who, perhaps, one particularly sad and hopeless morning, wakes up to find himself nine-days famous, just because he has called you — one of the many new names for progressive.

But such big dishonesty as this is, we will charitably hope, rare. Minor dishonesties,

THE LESSON OF ROMEIKE

such as allowing, say, the fact that a man was or was not at your college, and perhaps, indeed, never went to college at all — dear! dear! — insensibly to influence your review, are — well, let us be charitable, and call them merely human. Perhaps, too, the reviewer has heard about your blue and yellow hair, and can you blame him if he cannot quite forget it? A fellow may write as well or badly as you please, but, if he wears his hair blue and yellow, he must take the consequences. Probably it will not be dishonesty, but dulness and temperamental incapacity, with a consequent lack of any deep human experience, that will most bewilder you. You write of love, but your reviewer has never loved; of sorrow, but your reviewer has never known it. Then your book, with the imagination and the humour and the fancy, is all too likely to fall into the hands of a kindly enough fellow with none, or only one, or only two, of these qualities. What then? Well, again, nothing. You can soon tell for yourself if the man possesses imagination and humour and fancy, and if you decide not — well, his opinion is no affair of yours, and he has only done his duty in warning the people without imagination, humour, and fancy for whom he writes that your book is no affair of theirs. Never fear but your book will find its own, at last some day find its way with a little sigh into the hands that were meant to hold it. And you may rely on this, too, that whenever it shall have strayed into wrong hands awhile it will neither get nor give harm; for no one reads books against his will, and all books that really interest us are good for us. They bring something that we needed to help us grow, or keep us happy. And it is through such readers, who also have their representatives on the press, that you will learn the only lesson finally worth learning from Romeike: "in the scorn of circumstance" to be yourself and write for your own.

CONCERNING A DEFINITION OF POETRY

I HAVE just fallen a victim to the prevailing fashion and gone in for a *Times* reprint of the *Encyclopædia Britannica*, following the friendly recommendation of the publishers and choosing the half-morocco bound form, which, on comparison with a friend's cloth-bound copy, I find unquestionably superior and relatively cheaper. I have also gone in for a bookcase, and the whole investment is impregnating my bedroom with an essence of learning from which I am hopefully anticipating the most encouraging results. The other day I read in the papers the curious story of some sailors who had crossed the sea with a cargo of arsenic. For many weeks they had slept near to the arsenic, and the air they breathed was so full of it that these — possibly American — sailors grew fatter and fatter, till at length, on their arrival in port, their friends hardly knew them — they were so changed.

Now I am wondering if a similar intellectual fattening might not result from sleeping night after night in a room impregnated with *Encyclopædia Britannica*, and that is why I have had my copy placed in my bedroom. Then, apart from this unconscious method of assimilation, the little bookcase has a small reading-desk at its side, which is just about the right height for reading in bed; and the *Encyclopædia* may thus be used as an admirable "dormitive" for those who go to bed — but not to sleep. If, however, you desire a soporific you must not choose the article which has just stimulated me to a most enjoyable sleepless night. I should, of course, have read it long ago. That I did not was no fault of mine, for it was but natural that I tired at last of vain visits to the British Museum, to read an article in which I had heard would be found the very arcana of the greatest of all arts. The volume PHY— PRO was invariably in use, and it was evident that I was far from being the only one eager to read Mr. Theodore Watts-Dunton's famous

A DEFINITION OF POETRY

article on poetry. So at last I gave it up, and was compelled to write of poetry instructed only by my own instincts, a few ancient guides, and those admirable *Athenæum* reviews which, now that Mr. Watts-Dunton is vowed to romance, will, I suppose, grow even less frequent than they have been during the last five or six years. When, however, I saw the *Times* announcement of their reprint, I saw that my old desire might be fulfilled at last; and so, as some men marry an expensive wife for her smile, I have bought the *Encyclopædia Britannica* for Mr. Watts-Dunton's sake!

The article is worth the money. Its success is various, and it is a success such as an article of the kind can but rarely exemplify, a personal success. It is evidently the work of a poet, and, finally, no one who is not at least something of a poet himself has any authority as a critic of poetry. How dry-as-dust treatises on poetry usually are, how laboriously informing upon the superficialities, and how ignorant of the spiritual and sensuous springs deep down in the poet's nature! It has always been characteristic of

Mr. Watts-Dunton's *Athenæum* articles that he understands not only the psychology, but also the physiology of the poet, better than any other living English critic; and also that, while remaining a learned and even severe upholder of metrical laws, he has at the same time recognised that still higher law of instinct which in art is always liable to surprise us with incalculable and even forbidden successes. In regard to the ultimate basis of metre, I must allow myself quotation of this fine passage:—

"The rhythm of verse at its highest — such, for instance, as that of Shakespeare's greatest writings — is nothing more and nothing less than the metre of that energy of the spirit which surges within the bosom of him who speaks, whether he speak in verse or in impassioned prose. Being rhythm, it is, of course, governed by law, but it is a law which transcends in subtlety the conscious art of the metricist, and is only caught by the poet in his most inspired moods, — a law which, being part of nature's own sanctions, can of course never be formulated but only expressed, as it is expressed in the melody of the bird, in the inscrutable harmony of the entire bird-chorus of a thicket, in the whisper of the leaves of the tree, or in the song or wail of wind or sea."

A DEFINITION OF POETRY

It will be seen that those arbitrary distinctions which are often made between what one might call the Higher Prose and Poetry — and to which Mr. Watts-Dunton seems to subscribe in other parts of his article — are practically discountenanced in this passage.

In his definition of poetry: "Absolute poetry is the concrete and artistic expression of the human mind in emotional and rhythmical language," Mr. Watts-Dunton is perhaps more exact than his predecessors in that difficult experiment of definition. Yet should not a good definition possess, or suggest, some of the quality of the thing defined? And I am inclined to think that, compared with some earlier definitions, Mr. Watts-Dunton's definition loses in suggestiveness what it gains in exactitude. Not for a moment thinking to better so veritable an authority, but just throwing the phrase out as it chances to occur to me, I would venture to add this to the cairn of the definitions of poetry: *Poetry is that impassioned arrangement of words (whether in verse or prose) which embodies the exaltation, the beauty, the rhythm, and the pathetic truth of life.*

The article, of course, covers too much ground for one even to begin adequately to discuss it in a brief paper. I know not whether Mr. Watts-Dunton should be described as learned. I suppose in the pedantic jargon of the day, he would be discriminated from "a scholar" as a man, however, "of remarkably wide reading"—the word "scholar" apparently being reserved either for men who accumulate useless "learning," or for those who are unable to make any human use of their stores of really valuable knowledge. A wide reader, a deep thinker, a richly endowed humanist in the best sense, Mr. Watts-Dunton's article certainly proves him to be, and the manner in which he airily quotes Hindu writings "from memory" is calculated to dismay a generation more indolently nourished.

Perhaps the most interesting section of his article is that in which he discusses the two kinds of poetic imagination, or vision— "absolute vision," and "relative vision," or "dramatic imagination" and "egoistic" (or say, lyrical) "imagination." On this point I cannot help asking what always occurs to me in these discussions: Is dramatic imagina-

A DEFINITION OF POETRY

tion (however great and, indeed, pre-eminent, if you like) properly a branch of poetic imagination at all? Is not the coupling of them together merely a relic of the old association of drama with verse, an association finally dissolved in our day by the practice of at least one great master? Are not the poetic imagination and the dramatic imagination as essentially different from each other as, say, each is from the scientific imagination, to which, indeed, the dramatic imagination has perhaps greater affinity? When Homer and Shakespeare achieved those triumphs of absolute imaginative sight of their heroes at certain moments which Mr. Watts-Dunton adduces, they were not, I venture to submit, poets, but dramatists. A dramatist may be greater than a poet, but a dramatist and a poet are not the same thing, nor are they essentially related. They each see, as the scientist sees, but the three see such different things and in such different ways. I would ask, too, whether critics have not been in the habit of overrating this objective dramatic vision by forgetting what a comparatively common endowment it is. It is, of course, a great and wonderful quality, but some great modern novels surely possess it as remarkably as any of the ancient poets, and I would even go so far as to say, without any unworthy intention of flattery, that there are examples of it in Mr. Watts-Dunton's romance of "Aylwin" positively startling in their sense of absolute clairvoyance. That, indeed, is the quality which sets the book apart from the fiction of the day. But, great examples aside, is not the dramatic imagination — otherwise perhaps to be described as the realistic imagination — the gift sometimes of comparatively small, or at all events prosaic, writers? Few writers have surpassed Jane Austen in its possession, yet was there ever a more essentially prosaic writer?

THE DETHRONING OF STEVENSON

THE dethroning of Stevenson has begun. Though Stevenson almost accomplished the miracle of pleasing everybody, there was always — as in the case of Tennyson, and probably for a similar reason — a small party of depreciation. It was composed mainly of those whom we might call the secularists of literature, people in whom the reasoning and observing faculties of the intellect are angrily keen — the little "thinkers" and the little "realists" — and in whom such higher faculties of the intellect as imagination and the sense of beauty stertorously sleep.

During his lifetime these critics remained singularly voiceless. It was as though Stevenson had laid a charm upon them also. But Stevenson being dead — Mr. George Moore speaketh. Concerning the dead at all events let us have the truth — is Mr. Moore's version of *de mortuis*, and it is a version which one readily accepts, if only the truth be told with some of the gentleness which dictated the older, perhaps more human, version. Mr. Moore speaks a little disrespectfully of death — almost as disrespectfully as of Stevenson. One sees him a sort of Loki, who, when all the world is weeping for Stevenson, sits sulkily in his cavern and says: "No! I will not weep; I have wept for Balzac, but I will not weep for Stevenson. He could n't think, and he was no novelist. He could n't even write." Happily, Mr. Moore is a Loki whose criticism will keep no one out of Valhalla, least of all Stevenson; for Mr. Moore is always too angry when he differs for his criticisms to carry authority, though for Mr. W. B. Yeats' sake I shall hope that his praise is more important than his depreciation.

One will not deny that Mr. Moore had some reason to be a little out of temper. He cannot be the only one who is heartily sick of hearing every other new writer that comes along hailed as a new Stevenson, though his style and literary aims may be dissimilar to Stevenson's in every possible way. It is hard, too, on the writers thus distinguished. It handicaps them in the same way as the *sobriquet* of "the Belgian Shakespeare" has handicapped M. Maeterlinck. Besides, they may be humbly hoping some day to be themselves — not Stevenson nor another. We need go no further to illustrate the disadvantage of such irrelevant comparison than Mr. Moore's strictures on Stevenson *à propos* Mr. W. B. Yeats. No one had thought of comparing Mr. Yeats to Stevenson, however much they may have admired him. The genius of the one, a specialised imagination of delicate magic, a haunted fountain rising beneath the moon in fairyland, is so entirely unlike, either in quality or volume, to that of Stevenson. Yet when Mr. Moore, taking a descriptive passage from Mr. Yeats, challenges us to produce the like from Stevenson, the mere correction of the irrelevancy of the comparison has the look, unintentionally indeed, of depreciation towards the younger writer, not to speak of the risk of such a challenge being taken up. If Stevenson did one thing better than another it was his descriptions of night and early morning out of doors. The challenge is scarcely out of Mr. Moore's mouth before we have thought at least of the Princess's midnight flight through the woods in *Prince Otto*, with that magnificent mounting dawn — such pomp, such simplicity; and, of course, that unmatched night-piece in *Travels with a Donkey*. We so soon forget our old favourites in the new ones that Mr. Moore's excited blasphemies may possibly set some who have not read the donkey-book just lately wondering if Stevenson was really such a great writer after all. Let me, therefore, presume to refer them once again to a page I am thinking of.

But first let us quote the beautiful little passage from Mr. Yeats which Mr. Moore has somewhat cruelly subjected to so trying a comparison: —

"It was one of those warm, beautiful nights, when everything seems carved of precious stones. The woods of the Sleuth Hound away to the south looked as though cut out of green beryl, and the waters that mirrored them shone like opal. The roses he was gathering were like glowing rubies, and the lilies had the dull lustre of pearl. Everything had taken upon itself the look

STEVENSON DETHRONED

of something imperishable, except a glow-worm, whose faint flame burned on steadily among the shadows, moving hither and thither, the only thing that seemed alive, the only thing that seemed perishable as mortal hope."

Here is Stevenson: —

"Night is a dead, monotonous period under a roof; but in the open world it passes lightly, with its stars and dews and perfumes, and the hours are marked by changes in the face of Nature. What seems a kind of temporal death to people choked between walls and curtains is only a light and living slumber to the man who sleeps afield. All night long he can hear Nature breathing deeply and freely; even as she takes her rest she turns and smiles; and there is one stirring hour unknown to those who dwell in houses, when a wakeful influence goes abroad over the sleeping hemisphere, and all the outdoor world are on their feet. It is then that the cock first crows, not this time to announce the dawn, but like a cheerful watchman speeding the course of night. Cattle awake on the meadows; sheep break their fast on dewy hillsides, and change to a new lair among the ferns; and houseless men, who have lain down with the fowls, open their dim eyes and behold the beauty of the night. . . . When that hour came to me among the pines, I wakened thirsty. My tin was standing by me half full of water. I emptied it at a draught, and, feeling broad awake after this internal cold aspersion, sat upright to make a cigarette. The stars were clear, coloured, and jewel-like, but not frosty. A faint silvery vapour stood for the Milky Way. All around me the black fir-points stood upright and stock-still. By the whiteness of the pack-saddle, I could see Modestine walking round and round at the length of her tether; I could hear her steadily munching at the sward; but there was not another sound, save the indescribable quiet talk of the runnel over the stones."

Surely this is made out of silence. It is not so much writing as night itself. The difference between these two passages is simply that between a shell and a sea. However, it is a difference that one cannot well discuss without the risk, as I have said, of seeming to depreciate Mr. Yeats,— a risk which so true an admirer of his work as myself will not do himself the injustice of running. So fairy a thing as Mr. Yeats' genius should never have been storm-tossed on the angry breath of Mr. George Moore.

STEVENSON DETHRONED 157

But Mr. Moore's is not the only voice that is raised against Stevenson, though indeed it is in a very much milder spirit that Mr. St. Loe Strachey begs leave to put a question in some recently re-published essays. Mr. Strachey has discovered that there is something "that makes Mr. Stevenson's literary work never wholly satisfying," and is much concerned as to what it may be. He is evidently a great admirer of Stevenson all the same; there is quite an emotional ring about the more appreciative parts of his writing, and yet he cannot be content. There is a crumpled rose-leaf somewhere in his pleasure, and, like a true English critic, he can think of nothing but that. Faults first, merits afterwards! Such is our uncomfortable critical habit.

One is sorry for Mr. Strachey's sake that he never quite finds the offending rose-leaf to his own satisfaction. He is very confident at first that he has got hold of it, with the discovery that somehow or other Stevenson does not "edify." "We are finely touched" in Stevenson's writings, "but somehow not to fine issues!" Certainly this is the very last charge that we expected to be brought against Stevenson. Stevenson not good for the soul! Well, certainly this is a new Stevenson indeed. One had thought that if any writer had truly *edified* our younger generation it had been Stevenson. Certainly his was not a philosophy for old women or young ladies. No doubt it was a case of "port for men, brandy for heroes." But then neither men nor heroes are suckled on milk and soda. Then Mr. Strachey thinks that something "never wholly satisfying" may be, as Mr. George Moore thinks too, in his alleged incapacity to create living human beings. Yet for a bloodless puppet "Pinkerton" seems to have made a great impression on Mr. Strachey's quotations.

However, suppose one were to admit, what indeed the present writer was one of the first to say, that Stevenson has been overrated as a novelist — is there no other way of being a great writer than the way of *Esther Waters?* That Stevenson could tell certain stories and create certain characters is undeniable, but it is in his numerous other writings that his highest significance is to be found.

STEVENSON DETHRONED

And that significance is that of a poet using the medium of prose — a poet, and one of the most original philosophers of his time.

A philosopher! "Why, Stevenson could n't even think!" exclaim all the little "thinkers," who call a man a thinker only so long as his thoughts are hopelessly black or hopelessly tangled. To gain the reputation of profundity you must see, not with a clear, but with a troubled vision; you must not look through the veils, but lose yourself and your readers among them, crowding your page with subtle little studies of the various conflicting obfuscations that move smokily across the face of truth. When, however, a poet is able to transmute the crude materials of his philosophising into a lucent mysticism, minds unable to realise that there should be mystery in clearness mistake the profound azure of his thought for shallowness. Stevenson paid the penalty of thinking profoundly — that is, simply and hopefully — by being called shallow. More than any of our recent writers, he realised the unspeakable wonder of simplicity, "the mysterious face of common things." When a man like Maeterlinck makes just the same discoveries, but in a more oracular and much less brilliant style, he is saluted with awe as a mystic. Stevenson is only a charming essayist, with a pretty gift of fancy, but sadly thin in his ideas. Yet Stevenson was really a completer and more valuable mystic than any such men as Maeterlinck, valuable as M. Maeterlinck's beautiful writings are, for he added humour to his vision, and his mysticism was as all-embracing as his humanity. It was a daylight, not a moonlight mysticism, and was linked to no childish cult of fairies or Parisian sorcery, or to the neurasthenia of a dying Church. But I've said more than enough, I'm sure, to prove that Stevenson was no "thinker"!

A NEW WOMAN POET

NOT unaware of the wickedness of praising the new-born, and far from unaware of the perils of the praiser, I venture humbly to suggest to those interested in such matters that Miss Olive Custance's little volume of *Opals* contains the best poetry written by a woman for quite a long time. No one who knows the woman-poetry of the day can call this extravagant praise. Comparisons here are more than usually dangerous, and I shall venture on them no further than to express the opinion that the poetry written by women at the moment is full of talent but singularly lacking in temperament. It is profusely intellectual, definitely emotional, and infinitely spiritual. The expression of one's feelings in exact rhetoric is what, of course, many mistake for poetry, and women particularly make the mistake of supposing that there is nothing so easy as to put your heart on paper. The result is good love-letter, but mediocre poetry. To unlock the heart one needs a golden key, and the women are fewer than the men who sufficiently understand the mystery of words — understand that to put a thing into words, as we say, is not to rob it of its original mystery by a superficial clearness of statement, but actually to recreate it in another medium; and that, whatsoever qualities of mystery and indefinable suggestiveness belonged to the thing itself, must be repeated in its literary embodiment. Is it of spring we would write, there are words that were once violets, words as sad as the voice of the cuckoo; is it of woman — no woman was ever so beautiful as some words.

The face-value of words is but their least important value. Far more important is what we might call the nervous system of words: all that associated significance which thrills and vibrates beneath the printed surface. It is not what a line means, but what it suggests, that makes it poetry. However many meanings it may possess, the only meaning that really matters is the meaning of beauty — and what that is who shall say?

It must mean no more, but must mean no less, than the droop of an eyelid, the colour of a flower, or the sound of running water.

I am afraid that Miss Custance does not much trouble her head about literature and "the moral idea;" what is more to the purpose is that she instinctively understands some of the secrets of the use of words. The importance of her own moods, the exquisiteness and strangeness of living, the mystic beauty of the world, and all the glory and pathos it seems to mean in certain hours: music played at twilight, the sound of the rain, friends, and flowers (the friends as flowers, the flowers as friends), the sudden wonderful face of love, fair as a shooting star, her own beauty and the beauty of the morning sky, beautiful pain and all the mysterious sadness of joy — of such is the kingdom of earth for this young poet. And the words she finds for these moments are as rich and subtle, and yet as simple, as the moments themselves. Of one rare quality Miss Custance's poetry immediately asserts the possession, — the power of enrichment. Certain quite simple flowers and colours and textures possess this quality, but words possess it too seldom, for it is a sensuous quality; and though poetry that is simple and passionate is of not uncommon occurrence, poetry which fulfils the third Miltonic condition is rare. I have an idea that some critics believe this sensuous charm a common snare of the moment. As a matter of fact, however, it is just the quality in which the literature of the moment is singularly poor. Cleverness is everywhere, but where is enchantment? Are there half-a-dozen living English writers who possess this charm? It would be rash to say that there are, and no doubt it will sound still more rash to claim it for a little book by a very young poet. Yet, is it so rash after all to claim it for poetry such as this "Dreamed Tryst"?

" Beloved one! when the shy Dawn flower-sweet,
   In her white sleeping-gown of mist and pearl,
Sees the great Sun, and from her cloud-hung bed
   Slips softly, flushing like a startled girl,
And stands up-right on fair rose-coloured feet
   While all the golden light is round her shed . . .
'T is then that yearning, severed souls may meet . . .
   Slowly the glory widens in the sky
And in the meadows thick with folded flowers
   The daisies stir already in their sleep . . .

My soul lay waiting all the long night hours,
  But now thy promised presence hovers nigh,
In this still room I seem to hear the sweep
    Of thy soul's wings . . . O! Whither shall we fly?"

Or this — "A Pause";

"O! do you hear the rain
  Beat on the glass in vain?
  So my tears beat against fate's feet
  In vain . . . in vain . . . in vain . . .

"O! do you see the skies
  As gray as your grave eyes?
  O! do you hear the wind, my dear,
  That sighs and sighs and sighs . . .

". . . Tired as this twilight seems,
  My soul droops sad with dreams . . .
  You cannot know where we two go
  In dreams . . . in dreams . . . in dreams . . .

"You only watch the light,
  Sinking away from night . . .
  In silver mail all shadowy pale,
  The moon shines white, *so* white . . .

". . . O! if we two were wise
  Your eyes would leave the skies
  And look into my eyes!
  And I who wistful stand . . .
  One foot in fairy land,
  Would catch Love by the hand. . . ."

Among many reasons one might give for one's delight in these two poems, the reader must have noticed one, — the great beauty and truth of the Nature pictures. For descriptive magic alone Miss Custance's poems should rank high. And, like all her effects, this magic is won by such apparent simplicity of means. There is no sense of straining the eye upon the object. Just the flash of a phrase, and the miracle has happened. The picture is there, as though Nature had written her name in dewdrops. Who by taking thought could better give the beauty of rain than in these six simple words, —

> "A silver net of sudden rain"?

Miss Custance, like Verlaine, is a lover of the rain. Here are other rain pictures:

> "In the gray west a faint gold stain . . .
> Dusk and the darkness, sisters twain,
> Kiss through a silver veil of rain."

> "The gray west full of rain."

> "We catch stray scents from sweet drenched primrose stars —
> . . . And then the shower is over and rose-bars
> Bridge the sun's western garden and gold lake."

A NEW WOMAN POET

"Full of rain crystals, the asparagus
A jewelled tangle seems of strange green hair!"

In further illustration of Miss Custance's gift of beautiful and forcible phrase, particularly as applied to nature, I quote the following scattered lines and passages:

"Stars grow thick round the amber moon."

". . . . sun-soft summer air."

"Spirit of Twilight, in the golden gloom
Of dreamland dim, I sought for you and found
A woman weeping in a silent room
Full of white flowers that moved and made no sound."

"The hedges glimmer vaguely with wild fruits."

"The sky folds over like a flower,
Whose petal tips of purple gray
Flush flame-like at the sunset hour."

"Flushes of lingering colour, from afar
Reflect themselves in the round silver moon,
And in the blue burns flower-like one white star."

"Night lifts nearer luminous with stars."

"The wet trees toss their weight of tumbled green."

"Star-sandalled memories moving slow."

> "the red sun reels
> To other risings."
> "In her blue
> Bed-chamber, Morning loiters yet!"

And for a certain "large utterance" seldom heard in the poetry of women I would instance this beautiful river-picture:—

> ". . . In shadow of bent branches, let us go
> Down to the river side where rocks our boat
> Beneath the whispering willows. I will row
> And you shall steer . . . nay! rather let us float
> Tide-taken past the patient marigolds
> Whose dew-filled cups to Phœbus' self remote
> Are lifted up at Dawn. See! Day unfolds
> Her sunset robes refulgent in the West.
> Night's heavy lids that Light's strong hand upholds
> Droop low and hide the splendour. . . . Let us rest!"

One pleasant characteristic distinguishes Miss Custance from the typical woman poet, —she does n't pretend to be a man, but is quite consciously charmed with her own girlhood; though maybe one should not assume that the "frail girl in whom God's glories meet" of "The Poet's Picture" is necessarily the poet we are enjoying. Indeed her book, so to say, is a girl, a girl-poet, almost cruelly alive, experimentally passionate, tremulously sensitive to every sound straying across the Æolian harp of life. The little book seems to flush and tremble in one's hand. It is so exquisitely a girl.

It is girlish in its sadness, a luxurious sadness which is only a form of music, a way of dressing the hair, a wearing of "opals." "Opals" indeed describes these poems with an imaginative accuracy rare in titles: beautiful, troubled, distinguished, sad, fated, as opals. Girlish, yes — in everything but its art. One notes a very occasional carelessness, an extravagant and not always intelligible use of the French dot-and-dash ... pause and suggestion. "Shimmerous" is a word you can use too often — perhaps once even is too often. But, after all such criticisms are made, the spontaneous original charm, even power, of these "Opals" is undeniable. It has seldom happened that a young poet's first volume has been at once so full of beauty realised and so rich in promise of beauty to come.

MR. STEPHEN PHILLIPS'S POEMS

Mr. Stephen Phillips's poetry almost prompts one to the indiscretion of exclaiming, "A great poet at last!" At all events it is significant to note that he alone, of all the young poets at present qualifying for the great mantles thrown aside by their great predecessors of two generations ago, has been spared the impertinent label of "minor poet;" a nomination opprobrious because, as I have said before, it is used to-day in the sense of poetaster. So far as I have observed, no minor critic has yet dared to call Mr. Stephen Phillips a minor poet. Indeed, there seems to be a general sense abroad that here at all events is a poet who has got to be taken seriously, and whom it will be more than usually silly to deride. Therefore, in so fair a mood of the critical atmosphere, one may perhaps dare to whisper that in Mr. Stephen Phillips we have the first poet of his generation who gives promise of work which shall some day class him with the great Victorian poets. One who without presumption may perhaps claim to be an enthusiastic admirer of the poets of his own generation, may perhaps also be permitted the criticism upon them that they fall short, in comparison with such poets, say, as Keats, Tennyson, and Matthew Arnold, less in imagination and literary faculty than in humanity, and another power, which no doubt sounds very humble, and indeed perhaps hardly worthy, — the power to be interesting. I would not have them, like certain novelists, write for the great heart of the public, but I do regret that their distinguished, tuneful, charming, and even forcible numbers, should so seldom speak for the great heart of humanity — which is quite another matter. On all themes save the greatest and simplest they write with true inspiration. They have sung wonderfully of Wordsworth's poetry, of Irish fairies, of Catholic mysticism; but how often have they sung, say, even love, that stock-theme, with mastery or haunting magic? With the exception, perhaps, of "The Ballad of a Nun," "Mandalay," and

Mr. Dowson's less-known "Cynara," have they written one love-poem that it is impossible to forget, or even possible to remember? Nothing if not erotic, and yet not a genuine *cri du cœur* among them!

Where is their

"O that 't were possible,"

Or,
"He kissed
My soul out in a burning mist."

Ashamed of their feelings, lest some of Mr. Henley's prematurely aged young men should call them sentimental, and alarmed at their passions, in love-poetry at all events they have not prevailed.

But perhaps this is even too special a criticism, and a still more general test would be the test of beauty. The first duty of poetry is to be beautiful, and poetry is never supremely beautiful without being many other things too. This test our young poets bear somewhat better. Mr. Watson, at all events, has written some passages, such as the definition of peace in "Wordsworth's Grave," of noble and even haunting beauty.

PHILLIPS'S POEMS 173

Yet for the most part the beauty of our young poets' poetry is a rather special and literary beauty. Even their love of beauty is not quite a passion. Indeed, nothing is quite a passion with these young poets.

Not only do they lack passion, but they are also curiously lacking in pity and incapable of tenderness. In short, as I have said, they are, broadly speaking, lacking in humanity. Now, in this quality at its simplest and humanest Mr. Phillips's poetry is deeply rooted. However apparently remote his themes, whether they be a vision of Christ descending into hell, or a dream of Apollo contending in promises with the shepherd Idas for the maid Marpessa, they are immediately turned to a most poignantly human account. Take an example from the newer poem, these lines in which, with a charming womanliness, Marpessa gives one of the reasons for her rejection of the god: —

"O I
Should ail beside thee, Apollo, and should note
With eyes that would not be, but yet are dim,
Ever so slight a change from day to day
In thee my husband; watch thee nudge thyself

> To little offices that once were sweet:
> Slow where thou once was swift, remembering
> To kiss those lips which once thou could not leave.
> I should expect thee by the Western ray,
> Faded, not sure of thee, with desperate smiles,
> And pitiful devices of my dress
> Or fashion of my hair: thou wouldst grow kind;
> Most bitter to a woman that was loved.
> I must ensnare thee to my arms, and touch
> Thy pity, to but hold thee to my heart."

This might have been just "any wife to any husband." Then, too, her motherhood desires —

> "Passionate children, not
> Some radiant god that will despise me quite,
> But clambering limbs and little hearts that err."

Mr. Phillips feels in need of no subtle *nuance* or far-sought complexity in his subject-matter. Human life at its simplest is matter moving enough for him, and it is of the old truths of human feeling and experience that he makes his new beauty. For the storing of such experience he has a remarkably receptive and sympathetic eye, and it is perhaps rather the truth than the beauty of his poetry that first arrests one — or should one say that most of the beauty of his poetry

comes of its truth, which is another way of
saying that it is very fine poetry indeed?
This is certainly notable of the two most
original poems in his volume, "The Woman
with the Dead Soul," and "The Wife," whose
somewhat forbidding beauty, if one may be
allowed the term, almost entirely comes of
their union of accuracy and pity. By these
Stevenson's dictum, that the only realism
is that of the poets, is once more justified.
No prose realist with all the potent methods
of impressionism — not even Hubert Crackanthorpe — has given us such real pictures
of the London Inferno as Mr. Phillips
in the old-fashioned medium of the heroic
couplet. For the very detachment which
your professional realist attempts or affects
protects him from the reality. His failure is
to see that pity is part of the reality. In the
accuracy of his method Mr. Phillips reminds
one of Crabbe; in the mood of it, of Dante.
When one says that, it will be understood
that London has at last found a poet to sing
her seriously as a whole — not merely a poet
of her brothels. As an example of Mr.
Phillips's method at its best, one can only

quote once more this now oft-quoted passage from "The Wife":

"But at the door a moment did she quail,
  Hearing her little son behind her wail;
Who, waking, stretched his arms out to her wide,
  And softly, 'Mother, take me with you!' cried;
For he would run beside her, clasping tight
  Her hand, and lag at every window bright,
Or near some stall beneath the wild gas-flare,
  At the dim fruit in ghostly bloom would stare.
Toward him she turned, and felt her bosom swell
  Wildly: he was so young almost she fell
Yet took him up, and to allay his cries
  Smiled at him with her lips, not with her eyes,
Then laid him down; away her hand she snatched,
  And now with streaming face the door unlatched,
When lo, the long uproar of feet,
  The huge dim fury of the street!
While she into the wild night goes,
  That in her eyes a light shower blows.
Faces like moths against her fly,
  Lured by some brilliance to die:
The clerk with spirit lately dead,
  The decent clothes above him spread;
The joyous cruel face of boys;
  Those dreadful shadows proffering toys;
The constable with gesture bland
  Conducting the orchestral Strand;
A woman secretly distrest,
  And staidly weeping, dimly drest;

PHILLIPS'S POEMS

> A girl, as in some torment, stands,
> Offering flowers that burn her hands;
> A blind man passes, that doth sound
> With shaking head the hollow ground.
> In showering air, the mystic damp,
> The dim balm blown from lamp to lamp,
> A strange look from a shredded shawl,
> A casual voice with thrilling fall!"

Contributing to this reality of impression, if not indeed of the essence of it throughout Mr. Phillips's poetry, is his rare dramatic imagination, as apart from that more specially poetic imagination which makes "the little word big with eternity." Mr. Phillips seems to possess the psychological insight of a novelist, and perhaps the most marked example of this power is a lyric, before printed in the *Christ in Hades* volume, but in some danger of being missed among its more ambitious fellows, the lyric beginning with such poignant and masterly simplicity:—

> "I in the greyness rose;
>   I could not sleep for thinking of one dead.
>   Then to the chest I went,
>   Where lie the things of my beloved spread."

It is difficult to realise that a man could have written this poem without having undergone the experience it describes; and one of the closing lines, "A little jest, too slight for one so dead," is a wonderful revelation of the very heart of sorrow.

From the same power of the imagination which, as I have before said, is little short of clairvoyance, proceeds Mr. Phillips's power of picture-making — such pictures as —

"Lonely antagonists of destiny
That went down scornful before many spears;"

or

"The bright glory of after-battle wine,
The flushed recounting faces, the stern hum
Of burnished armies. . . ."

Talk of impressionism! What can the most skilful and curious of French impressionists do more victoriously vivid than two such pictures as are contained in the last ten words? Keats used to say that poetry was mainly an affair of adjectives. For poetry following Latin models the dictum certainly holds, and Mr. Phillips's is obviously made exclusively on Latin models. But, if some poetry be mainly an affair of adjectives, and some an affair of feeling, Mr. Phillips is equally happy in his gifts. I have spoken of that beauty in Mr. Phillips's poetry which is truth to piteous things, but it must not be thought that Mr. Phillips is less sensitive to the beauty of the joy and the bounty and the magnificence of life. If to transmute those piteous things into beauty is one of the great offices of the poet, it is no less his privilege to be the mirror of that fair face of the world which asks no added beauty from any poet — and to that face no other poet of his generation has held up so lovely a mirror as "Marpessa." By this time the love-speech of Idas is already a classic by much quotation, and hardly less familiar is the splendid flash and thunder of the passage in which Apollo pictures "We two in heaven running;" therefore, I will quote instead this no less memorable passage, in which Marpessa answers Apollo: —

"Then, thou speak'st of joy,
Of immortality without one sigh,
Existence without tears for evermore.
Thou would'st preserve me from the anguish, lest
This holy face into the dark return.
Yet I, being human, human sorrow miss.

The half of music, I have heard men say,
Is to have grieved; when comes the lovely wail
Over the mind; old men have told it me
Subdued after long life by simple sounds.
The mourner is the favourite of the moon,
And the departing sun his glory owes
To the eternal thoughts of creatures brief,
Who think the thing that they shall never see.
Since we must die, how bright the starry track!
How wonderful in a bereavéd ear
The Northern wind; how strange the summer night,
The exhaling earth to those who vainly love.
Out of our sadness have we made this world
So beautiful; the sea sighs in our brain,
And in our heart that yearning of the moon.
To all this sorrow was I born, and since
Out of a human womb I came, I am
Not eager to forego it; I would scorn
To elude the heaviness and take the joy,
For pain came with the sap, pangs with the bloom:
This is the sting, the wonder."

It is not too much to say that no such poem as "Marpessa" has been written since Keats abandoned "Hyperion" — for a reason that, evidently, would not dismay Mr. Phillips.

TRAGEDY AND MR. WILLIAM WATSON

(*À Propos* Mr. William Watson on "Tragedy and Mr. Stephen Phillips" in *The Fortnightly Review*.)

THERE is, I hope, and certainly Mr. Watson knows, no need for me to preface my remarks with any such confession of delight in poetical gifts which all acknowledge, as that which makes such a graceful exordium to Mr. Watson's criticism of Mr. Phillips. Still I may be permitted to record a reminiscence similar in shape to his of a night, I fear almost ten years ago, when I too sat with a distinguished friend, he and I "talking about our beloved poets until far into the waning night" and "how at last I managed to make the discovery that," while he knew most poets worth knowing, if indeed he did n't quite know "everything under the sun" — it is admitted that no reader but Mr. Churton Collins knows that — "he was ignorant of the name and work of " — Mr. William Watson.

It chanced that that very day I had picked up a copy of the *National Review*, containing " Wordsworth's Grave," and the poem had been singing in my head all evening. So we shared the new-found treasure on the spot. If I had a sovereign for all the times I have recited some of the stanzas since then, I should be a rich man.

To admire Mr. Watson as a poet is, from the nature of the material which he knows best how to employ, to respect him as a critic too. No better literary criticism than "Wordsworth's Grave" has been written in England for a long while. *Excursions in Criticism* confirmed this, though here the prose was perhaps better than the criticism, which had a tendency to be academic, and to rely too much on eighteenth-century canons of form and taste. Mr. Watson seemed to consider that literary criticism ended with Dr. Johnson. What would the good doctor think of Rossetti? he asked — as if there could be the smallest critical profit in measuring the work of one man by the taste of another so radically dissimilar. Dr. Johnson was, of course, — Dr. Johnson; but for that very delightful reason he is entirely inadequate as a critic of nineteenth century poetry. Unless literature of all human things is to be doomed to unprogressive imitation of the masters, we must have critics who keep pace with its developments; and whoever thinks that art stopped short in the cultivated court of the Empress Josephine, or at any other point of its history, may make delightful prose out of his anachronistic prepossessions, but must not complain if we regard him as a blind guide of much accomplishment and charm.

Now Mr. Watson's criticism of Mr. Stephen Phillips is distinctly Johnsonian. Mr. Phillips' poetical powers are not in the balance,— of those Mr. Watson makes a most generous recognition. It is in Mr. Phillips' conception of, and Mr. Watson's definition of, tragedy that the Johnsonian character of Mr. Watson's mind is revealed with startling clearness. Mr. Watson is all the time thinking of tragedy as a form, Mr. Phillips as an essence — and just in that lies the difference between the old and the new conceptions of tragedy. Actually Mr. Watson's objection to the application of the word tragedy to Mr. Phillips' grim London poems, "The Woman with the Dead Soul" and "The Wife" are no more radically pertinent than if he had declared them no tragedies because they were not written in five acts, and paid no proper regard to the unities.

Mr. Watson, with specious plausibility, declares that "the very essence of tragedy" lies in "the overthrow of something great," proceeding to instance as examples of "something great," certain spectacular Shakespearean kings, and to object against Mr. Phillips' poor tragédiennes of the gutter, with a curious shallowness of sympathy, and cynicism of regard for a poet, that there was originally nothing great in them to overthrow. "*In these insignificant and immemorable human lives*," he says in a passage which perhaps hardly needs the italics I give it, "*no material of tragedy exists; these trivial and microscopical individualities do not provide the theatre in which alone may tragedy be enacted.*" How strangely that sounds in a modern ear! One wonders what the dramatist of *Ghosts* would think of the statement, and of this which complements it : "Tragedy demands as the prime condition of its presentment, a moral stage of some grandeur and amplitude. A great or splendid spirit is wrecked, or overborne, or gradually disintegrated, and in the terror of such a spectacle there is sublimity and awe. If a palace or a fortress fall, we tremble; we do not stand aghast at the collapse of a mud hut." How feudal and generally reactionary is the temper of Mr. Watson's mind, his imagery alone bears witness. Surely it depends entirely on the spectator, the human issues involved, and the power of the dramatist, that relative tragedy of palace, fortress, or mud hut. If Ibsen undertook the tragedy of the mud hut we should tremble fast enough, as were he to undertake the tragedy of the castle and fortress, so impressive from the outside, he would be able to show, as likely as not, the essential meanness and unsublimity, too squalid for tragedy, of their crashing and picturesque fall.

Mr. Watson has failed to see that such stories as that of Macbeth are not specially tragic material, but have only come to seem so through the power of the great poet who so piercingly saw and picturesquely embodied their tragedy. Essentially Macbeth and his wife were no more significant and memorable lives than those which Mr. Phillips sings. Had we read of them elsewhere than in Shakespeare, we should have seen in them little more than two middle-class murderers for mean objects, as virtually they were. Such a story as theirs is, essentially, less tragic than the story of such a sacrifice as that told by Mr. Phillips in "The Wife," less tragic if for no other reason than that it is more vulgar. A pure woman who in great agony of soul, and with a terrible consciousness of moral degradation, sells her body to buy food for her dying husband! Surely there is a tragic enough world for Mr. Watson's theatre, a sufficiently crushing sense of the overthrow of something great. To murder an old king for his money — virtually, call it his kingdom if you prefer — and then walk in your sleep with horror, and be executed in battle for your vulgar crime by one of his relations, is almost too bloody to be tragic. I confess that to me no crimes of those ancient capitalists of stolen cattle we call kings, can compare in tragic, or even merely dramatic, significance with such a story.

It is true they are more spectacular, and if tragedy were a matter of blood and drums, Mr. Watson would be right, but latterly tragedy begins to convince just in proportion as it is less spectacular and more spiritual. To certain people the "death of a peer" on the placard of some evening paper seems to lend death an impressiveness they had forgotten for it awhile, and the doings of the rich must from the material conditions of life receive a momentary notoriety; but this is all snobbery and vulgarity of spirit, and finally it is neither station nor wealth that makes the tragic theatre or the tragic figure, but the intensity of the vital, not necessarily moral, issue, involved in any given situation of howsoever socially insignificant human beings.

"These insignificant and immemorable human lives!" "These trivial and microscopical individualities"! Surely this is not the poet of Armenia that is talking. It sounds much more like his favourite Sultan! Certainly it was in a moment of deeper insight that Mr. Watson once wrote:

> "Momentous to himself as I to me
>   Hath each man been that ever woman bore;
> Once, in a lightning-flash of sympathy,
>   I *felt* this truth an instant, and no more."

Evidently that instant is over, and it must have been in another moment of singular insensitiveness to the mysterious spiritual significance and destiny of human life, not merely in its conspicuous action, sunlit or lightning-struck, but *en masse*, that Mr. Watson permitted himself to write so contemptuously of the unlaurelled, inglorious majority.

Who is he, or I, or anyone, that we should talk of "these insignificant and immemorable human lives! These trivial and microscopical individualities"! It is true, of course, as he says, that there are great things and little things in this world, and that all men and women are not equally important, but it needs an insight no more profound than that of any Christian, to realise that the least "important" human soul is a being of entirely mysterious responsibilities and destinies, and that on the

TRAGEDY

smallest needle-point of personality there is room for one knows not what angels and devils to dance.

No, Mr. Stephen Phillips has heard the "still sad music of humanity," as even Wordsworth's laureate seems not to have heard it; and it is just that humanity, in which, as I have said before, lies his superiority to his contemporaries. In "Marpessa" even it is the humanity more than the beauty that impresses one, and it is just his almost painful sensitiveness to the strange joy and sorrow of human life which made him realise the spiritual terror of a soul, any soul — what matter whose! — that could slowly die to all the wonder of the world —

> "all the dew,
> Tremble, and suddenness of earth."

A common woman, materialised out of all her spiritual instincts, deaf and blind to the immortal singing and shining of existence, may not seem to every one a tragic figure; perhaps it depends on how alive one is oneself, how keenly one feels the tragedy of such a death-in-life. That Mr. Phillips with his spiritual vision, his rich senses, and his warm pity, should feel such a tragedy with a personal keenness was to be expected. We shall feel it with him in proportion as we feel anything, and realise with him the "something great" overthrown in proportion as we value the individual human soul. Any human soul in agony, or in stupor — that for some of us seems a sufficiently tragic spectacle.

À PROPOS THE BROWNING LOVE-LETTERS

ONE is thankful for the spirit in which these letters have been generally received by the critics. When poor Mr. Buxton Forman ventured to publish the much less intimate and less passionate letters of Keats, the reception of his " indiscretion " was very different. In fact he has never, I fancy, heard the last of it. There has, however, been a general disposition gratefully to condone Mr. Browning's gift to the nation of the *cor cordium* entrusted to him by his great parents, — or rather, more strictly speaking by his great father. Robert Browning had kept these letters, carefully numbered and in order, in an inlaid box, and not long before his death, having destroyed all the rest of his correspondence, he spoke to his son, referring to them : " There they are, do with them as you please when I am dead and gone ! " It is evident that Browning loved his love-story, and loved the world to love it too. All natural, unconventionalised men do. The man who has grown a rose, or discovered a star, does not hasten to hide the fact as a rule; on the contrary, he calls in his friends to festival and says: "Rejoice with me." There is at least so much generosity in human nature. He does not say: "This rose is too sacred, or this star too sacred for other eyes to look upon;" but on the contrary: "This rose, this star, is *so* sacred that I must not keep it for my selfish eyes alone. Rather is it my duty to reveal it to the whole world, that the eyes of all men may be blessed by this wonder, and their hearts purified." The holy sacraments are not profaned by being lifted up in the eyes of the people. It is the people who are sanctified. Beautiful holy things can never be profaned from without. If the great love-stories of the world had been kept "private," as some smug old-maidish critics would, no doubt, prefer, how impoverished the world would be.

One has often heard on these occasions that great writers do not, by the accident of fame, forfeit their rights as private persons. Of course, within certain obvious limitations they do not. We do not expect to watch them eating their every meal in a glass-house in Trafalgar Square. Nor do we expect them to sleep in public. And, of course, if they like to insist upon them, all such remaining rights of private persons as they can retain are theirs. But this does not alter the fact that a great writer is not a private person, no more or no less so than her Majesty the Queen. Certain critics love to affect the "Mr." before great names. Mr. Lang, I fancy, still speaks of "Mr. Arnold," meaning Matthew Arnold, as he would name any other private gentleman. But then Matthew Arnold is no longer a private gentleman, and never will be any more. You might as well say "Mr. Burns" or "Herr Heinrich Heine." Matthew Arnold and Burns and Heine and the two Brownings are no longer mere men and women, but types of the human spirit, and as much public property as the Venus of Milo, or the portrait of Andrea del Sarto by himself. It is sheer snobbish affectation to deem otherwise.

It is the duty of every great man to bequeath his love-letters to the British Museum, and Robert Browning, through his son, has beautifully fulfilled that duty. That Mrs. Browning does not appear to have been consulted, — though there is no reason to suppose that her husband was without knowledge of what her wishes would be in such an event — need not, it seems to me, make us uncomfortable. It is true that she herself, though the most impulsive and open-hearted of poets, was paradoxically so reticent of her own personal feelings as not to be able to reveal her "Portuguese" sonnets to her husband till after her marriage, as too for a long while she was unable to endure the thought of their appearance in print. At the same time it must be remembered that her ill-health, and the cloistered circumstances of her home, had made her morbidly sensitive in social life. She shrank from meeting new faces, and we read in these letters how long it took her to brace herself to receive face to face one who already before their first meeting had become an intimate correspondent. Perhaps, similarly, it was her invalid life that accounts for her timorous attitude towards the absurd tyranny of her father, who, though she was a woman already in the thirties, pecuniarily independent of him, and world-famous, restricted her liberty in selfish petty ways difficult to conceive. Then too love had come late to her, and there is no one so maidenly as a woman on the borders of old maidenhood. Often in reading her letters one wonders how Browning had "patience" with her — particularly in her submission towards her father. One longs to see him, like Mr. Meredith's Alvan, carry her off "on the back of a centaur." For, it must have been evident to him almost from the beginning that she loved him all the time. In any case, therefore, I should hold that Mrs. Browning's scruples, supposing her to have had any, might have been reverently and affectionately disregarded, in favour of the robuster, more natural will of her husband. Even here too father and son have done well.

It has, I see, been objected that virtually these letters add nothing to the Browning love-story as already known to us. The poetry on each side had already told us all.

That is in a sense true; but, on the other hand, while poetry tells us everything, it tells us nothing. Even in its most intimate moments it becomes generalised. In its application it is always "any man to any woman," rather than the particular man to a particular woman. An advantage, of course, in some ways; but in a sense a loss in humanity. However real words may be in themselves, they seem more real when we know them to be the real utterances of real people. The world in general especially feels this, and is apt to distrust the sincerity of verse. Therefore, a volume of prose letters is in its eyes better evidence of a great love than the most wonderful series of sonnets (poets have such a way of exaggerating their feelings!) — and it is very important, allowing the importance of any thing, that the world should be convinced of such matters. In the poetry we hear the two poets in love. It is the loves of the angels. It is the morning stars singing together. But here in plain — though often obscure — prose, we hear the man and woman in love, in love like mere men and women, in spite of all their references to the *Agamemnon* and the *Prometheus* — for surely these are the most learned lovers that ever loved. The world thrills at: "How do I love thee, let me count the ways," but, almost terrible in its pathetic sincerity as that cry is, perhaps the world is more convinced by such simple prose as this which simple and unknown women have written over and over again from the beginning: "My own dearest, — what would become of me indeed, *if* I could not see you on Wednesday, nor on Thursday, nor on Friday? — no breath I have for going on. No breath I should have, for living on. I do kiss you through the distance — since you tell me. I love you with my soul. Your own I am." Or again: "It seems to me still a dream how you came here at all, ... the very machinery of it seems miraculous. Why did I receive you and only you? Can I tell? No, not a word." Or once more: "And for the rest, you need not fear any fear of mine — my fear will not cross a wish of yours, be sure! Neither does it prevent your being all to me ... all: more than I used to take for all when I looked round the world ... almost more than I took for all in my earliest dreams. You stand in between me and not merely the living who stood closest, but between me and the closer graves . . . and I reproach myself for this sometimes, and, so, ask you not to blame me for a different thing."

À PROPOS "THE ABSENT-MINDED BEGGAR"

"The Absent-Minded Beggar," that wonder-working capitalised lyric has no warmer admirer in England than the present writer. I hum it in season and out of season. I have risked the displeasure of near and dear relatives for my love of it. "And yet—" as Mr. Stephen Phillips says in one of his lyrics, "and yet—" Well, you see, one's own personal unregenerate delight is one thing; what I have been pondering is another. Personally, I have rejoiced in Mr. Kipling's ballad as I have rejoiced — and the whole of England with me — in any other preposterously fascinating catch from the music hall, say, "The Man That Broke the Bank at Monte Carlo," or "Ta-ra-ra-boom-de-ay." But the very nature of my delight leads me to ask what I conceive to be a pertinent question. England, we must remember, is not only an old and rich country, but it is the most "distinguished" country in the world. So far as one can generalise on such matters, England — and certainly France no longer — is the gentleman among the nations. It is not merely the wealth of England that has caused its manners to be lovingly copied all over the world. Well, taking the great distinction of England for granted, is it at a great national crisis adequately represented by — the music hall? And when England goes forth to battle, is it seemly that her war song should be written in the dialect of Cockney coster-mongers? Truly national poetry is not written in the slang of a nation's slums. When France needs a new national song it will not commission Aristide Bruant to write it.

For, of course, Cockney is not to be considered on the same plane of dialect as Scotch dialect. Scotch dialect represents a nation. Every Scotchman is born to it, and he is seldom able to sell his birthright. A Scotch national song written in plain English would be as inappropriate — as an English national song written in Cockney. English is a noble and beautiful language. We have still amongst us poets who can use it nobly and beautifully. We don't send Mr. Arthur Roberts to represent us at international conventions; why, then, in front of our armies should we send a Cockney Taillefer? Let Whitechapel have its "Absent-Minded Beggar" by all means — but Whitechapel is only a small corner of the English constitution, and Mr. Kipling's genius is not great enough to elevate a gutter-slang into a national speech.

That we are willing at the moment to accept a music-hall song in lieu of a really national poem is a fact, I fear, of no good import. Remembering Tennyson's noble and dignified ballads and odes on such occasions, one cannot be altogether happy that England, with the echo of such distinguished music in its ears, can rest content with "The Absent-Minded Beggar." A fact, I said, of no good import, — indeed, of discouraging import on many sides! Those of us who have believed in democracy cannot but ask ourselves: Is this what democracy means? Many wise heads have prophesied that democracy would mean just this: brutalisation of the national conscience, vulgarisation of the noble arts. We have hesitated to believe it — and perhaps even yet we need not believe it true. Democracy, like an army, has a way of persuading aristocrats to lead it. To take one example: William Morris, in spite of all his abstract "equality," was by temperament an aristocrat; and maybe we have been too apt to interpret the democratic movement by such leaders, forgetting that democracy above all should be read not by its few illuminated letters, but by the general purport of its average page. It is something of a paradox that a so-called aristocratic, "Tory" movement, such as our latest "imperialism," should come to be led by a man who is not, in any sense of the word, an aristocrat; neither by birth, temperament, taste, nor achievement, — and that its most forcible expression of itself should be made in the plebeian dialect of the lowest classes. If it is important that "gentlemen" — using the word in its full sense — lead us in battle, it is even more important that "gentlemen" should decide for what reasons, or to what issues, those battles should be fought; and

ABSENT-MINDED BEGGAR

also that "gentlemen"—that is, the select natures of literary art—should sing our battle songs. If the coster is to make England's wars—that is, if England is to be managed by its most common and least instructed citizens—then, and only then, is it appropriate that its poets should voice the national feeling in coster dialect. It is to be feared that, for all his Tory sentiments, Mr. Kipling does indeed represent in literature the "average, sensual" elector, whose comprehension of a national crisis depends on its effect upon his particular industry. What a humiliation for poetry! Of old the poet sat high above the herd upon the sacred hill, and the herd looked up to him, as a vessel of the divine meanings. Clumsily it strove to attain comprehension of his universal prophetic outlook upon the world. But with Mr. Kipling, the poet has changed all that. No longer he sits aloof, an intermediary between God and the mob; but, instead, he runs eagerly down the hill, the willing phonograph of the greatest number.

The mob has found a man of genius willing to voice its prejudice and rapacity. This is bad for England, and very humiliating for poetry. It almost makes one wish that poetry were constituted as a faculty, like medicine, and that there were certain unprofessional things clearly defined which a poet might not do. Of course, if England is satisfied to be represented by the "Absent-Minded Beggar," all the worse for England; it only means that its finer minds are withdrawing themselves from the direction of the national destiny.

Yet, on the other hand, all this is not to say that the "Absent-Minded Beggar" is anything but a fascinating human jingle. There are those who consider it a slur upon the English soldier. He is not an absent-minded beggar — say some. Of course, that is absurd. And there is underneath the surface cynicism of Mr. Kipling's poem a frank acceptance of humanity as it is, which is in itself humanising. Yet I maintain that, whatever its secondary charm, however, individually, one may delight in it, the "Absent-Minded Beggar" is unworthy to represent so great and so distinguished a country as England at such a moment.

There are those, I know, who consider such doggerel an indication of the future of English literature. The poetry of the twentieth century is to be just Kipling — only more so. Of course, one cannot deny or affirm. One can only hope not — and look to the past for consolation. This, of course, is not the first time that English national feeling has expressed itself in plebeian jingle. There was, for instance, a certain "Lillibullero," which every duke's son and cook's son in eighteenth-century England hummed in a sort of possession. It hums now only in the dry heads of antiquaries. And there is the sadness of Mr. Kipling's talent; or, perhaps, rather the use to which he has chosen to dedicate that talent. Think of "Mandalay" as the dusty property of literary dry-as-dusts. Yet, what else can it become? Mr. Kipling has chosen to make the clay jig, instead of compelling the marble to sing; and he has his reward. To-night as, all unexpectedly, I caught my train, I noticed a gentleman walking about the well-covered railway station with his umbrella up. It was raining outside, and he had forgotten to put the umbrella down. Said a porter to me: "There goes an absent-minded beggar," and for a moment I thought to myself: "What a fame is that which is breathed upon the lips of railway porters!" — till I remembered the fame of prize-fighters and pantomime songs; and thought, too, of Keats! "What think you of Keats?" I might have said to my porter. Yes! if Mr. Kipling troubles himself about "immortality" — as every real artist should — he must turn pale at the thought of Keats. Of course, it is impossible to imagine the "Ode to a Grecian Urn" making fifty thousand pounds for our widows and orphans; — "and yet . . ."

HUBERT CRACKANTHORPE

In Memoriam.

For a little while, no doubt, idle conjecture will still busy itself with the mysterious fate of Hubert Crackanthorpe, but for those who knew and loved him, that mystery is now merged in a greater, which "this side the stars" no man may read. We ask no longer why and how he died — we can only say over to ourselves that he is surely dead. A little urn, which faith and love would fain hide from us with symbolic flowers of resurrection, and three little books are all that is left to us of one who but yesterday was so vividly and endearingly alive. That he has left us thus of his free will, without a word of adieu, without a wave of the hand, is hard to think: for that were indeed "all unlike his great and gracious ways." A gentleman so gentle, a man so human, a heart so tender, a nature so noble and true — it was so we spoke of him day by day as he lived. May one who loved him, and to whom he was so rare a friend, say it once more now that he is dead? I have spoken of him " so vividly and endearingly alive," and it is just this which for him, and such as he, adds bitterness even to the bitterness of death — he loved life so well, and it was so good a sight to see him alive, so eagerly, so passionately, and with so vast and sympathetic a humanity.

> " I must
> Remember young men dead in their hot bloom,
> The sweetness of the world edged like a sword."

Humanity. It was that word which significantly he wrote in the forefront of his first book with the terrible title of *Wreckage*, and humanity was ever the motto of Hubert Crackanthorpe's life. He was inexhaustibly interested in men and women, and the pity of their terrible destinies, and perhaps hardly another writer of his generation had so thoroughly equipped himself for his calling of novelist by so adventurous a study of human life. Like Browning's poet, his dreams were of

> " Marts, theatres, and wharfs — all filled with men!
> Men everywhere!"

But the study was always first for its own sake, for the love and the pity of it, and only secondarily for the making of books. Indeed, that was far from being first among his interests, and I well remember from our last talk his eloquent protestation that always in literature the man was so much more to him than the book. His estimation of his own writings was more than modest, it was unaffectedly indifferent. When he wrote, he wrote with all his might and skill; but, for all the praise and expectancy which his work had won for him, he remained true to that "pursuit of experience" which, half pathetically and half ironically maybe, he has declared "the refuge of the unimaginative;" and flattery, that left his ambitions as it found them, left, too, his nature sincere and unspoiled.

To him, of all men, it would seem trivial in such an hour of parting to attempt estimate of the value of his contributions to literature, or of the loss to literature by his death; and surely I propose no such attempt here; but though he might think so little of them himself, we shall know how to value the three volumes where alone henceforth we may meet his gentle and heroic spirit. And I think it is not friendship that blinds me when I venture to believe that posterity will deem the youth who could write *Wreckage* at the age of twenty-two something like the Chatterton of the English novel. It is seldom that so young a man is so objective in his method, so capable of getting outside himself, of seeing with so faithful a vision, and recording with so minute a reality, the psychology of temperaments different from his own. " Unimaginative," indeed, the writer of that wonderful story, *A Dead Woman*, was far from being; indeed, the dramatic imagination necessary to the writing of such a story might almost seem to transcend imagination and become actual clairvoyance. The hearts of the tragic, of the desperate ones, have seldom found a more understanding and sympathetic interpreter; and now among the histories of those for whom he had so vast a pity his own sad history has come to be written. Memories not unacquainted with sorrow will scarcely recall so pitiless an ending of so promising a life, but among the treasures of such memories there

HUBERT CRACKANTHORPE

will not be a memory more dear and beautiful than that of Hubert Crackanthorpe. I said he had left us no farewell, and yet as one reads the closing words of his last book, does it not seem as though, unconsciously, he was already bidding us good-bye?

"Have you never longed to wander there, in that wonderful cloudland beyond the sea, where, like droves of monstrous cattle, close-huddled and drowsy, they lie the day through — the comely, milk-white summer clouds, slow and sleek and swelling; . . . sometimes, at evenfall, when the sea lies calm in her opal tints, you may discern the distant lines of their strange, fantastic home, vague, phantasmagoric, like a mirage beyond the horizon.

"Perhaps, after death, we may linger there, and watch them silently sail away towards the lands we have loved long ago! . . ."

Perhaps, who knows?